REAL MEN

TEN COURAGEOUS AMERICANS TO KNOW AND ADMIRE

R. CORT KIRKWOOD

CUMBERLAND HOUSE
NASHVILLE, TENNESSEE

REAL MEN

PUBLISHED BY CUMBERLAND HOUSE PUBLISHING, INC

431 Harding Industrial Drive

Nashville, Tennessee 37211

Cover design by Gore Studio, Inc., Nashville, Tennessee

Library of Congress Cataloging-in-Publication Data

Kirkwood, R. Cort.

Real men : ten courageous Americans to know and admire / R. Cort Kirkwood.

    p. cm.

Includes bibliographical references.

ISBN-13: 978-1-58182-563-3 (pbk. : alk. paper)

ISBN-10: 1-58182-563-3 (pbk. : alk. paper)

    1. Heroes—United States—Biography. 2. Courage—United States. I. Title.

CT215.K57 2005

920.02—dc22   2006020947

Printed in the United States of America

1 2 3 4 5 6 7 8 9 10—10 09 08 07 06

R. Cort Kirkwood's *Real Men* is long overdue. Over and against the aimless and emasculated man of American popular culture, Kirkwood offers us men of true character—of courage, bravery, and honor—for our emulation. Young men in particular need to read *Real Men*, since it will force them to make a choice: do I wish to live as a self-absorbed hedonist, as MTV advises, or do I wish to be a man? After reading this book, men of all ages will be inspired by these great models—and more insulted than ever by the helpless and effeminized nobodies that feminists and other leftists have dared to offer in their place.

—Professor Thomas Woods
Author, *The Politically Incorrect Guide to American History* and *The Great Facade: Vatican II and the Regime of Novelty in the Roman Catholic Church*

Kirkwood has written a joyful masterwork of political incorrectness, a highly readable celebration of the masculine virtues of American heroes from Audie Murphy to Vince Lombardi.

—Terence P. Jeffrey
Syndicated Columnist
Editor, *Human Events*

R. Cort Kirkwood's new book highlights patriotic masculinity and should be a highly prized addition to the library of every American ready to learn from examples of historically correct, if politically unfashionable, character and leadership.

—Howard Phillips
Chairman, Conservative Caucus

From our vantage point at CWA, we know there are many, many mothers and fathers out there who are yearning to see their sons influenced by the kind of men that R. Cort Kirkwood brings to life in *Real Men*. In this book, we find stories of faith, courage, and determination. America has had more than its share of heroes, even if most textbooks no longer honor them. *Real Men* is a stunning reminder of the caliber of men that America must raise up if we are to remain a self-governing, free people blessed by God.

—Beverly LaHaye,
Founder and Chairman, Concerned Women for America

In an age when the "metrosexual" male is offered as a role model to boys, R. Cort Kirkwood's fine book about ten American men is a welcome antidote. Did you know that Wild Bill Hickok really did have all those shoot-outs? Or that Lou Gehrig broke seventeen bones in his hand over the years but would not miss a game? Kirkwood's easy narratives are packed with nuggets like these. It's a fine read, and it would make a great gift for boys out there who are hungry for heroes. As a guy working for the women's organization that likes men and expects them to act accordingly, I heartily endorse *Real Men* for all readers—especially boys.

—Robert Knight
Director of the Culture and Family Institute,
an affiliate of Concerned Women for America,
and author of *The Age of Consent: The Rise of Relativism and the Corruption of Popular Culture*

REAL MEN

For my children

Lauren Elizabeth

Kelly Ann

Samuel Jordan

Robert Sean

Caroline Brooke

Mary Katherine

CONTENTS

ACKNOWLEDGMENTS

My thanks to the following kind men and women who helped with this book:

To Terence P. Jeffrey, editor of *Human Events;* Beverly La-Haye and Robert Knight of Concerned Women for America and the Culture and Family Institute; Jeff Mellott, staff writer for the *Harrisonburg (Va.) Daily News-Record;* Howard Phillips of the Conservative Caucus and historian Thomas Woods for reading the manuscript and lending their support.

To historian Roger McGrath for reading the manuscript and contributing the foreword.

To Ron Pitkin, Ed Curtis, Tracy Ford, and the staff of Cumberland House.

To the men who inspired not only generations of Americans but also this book.

And to my lovely and wonderful wife, Dana, who, with the heroes in these pages, helped teach me what it means to be a real man.

FOREWORD

Ever since the late 1960s the cultural Marxists of academe have worked assiduously to destroy American heroes or to simply omit them from textbooks—and they have done a good job. Most young Americans today know nothing of Francis Marion, Eddie Rickenbacker, or Audie Murphy and next to nothing about Andrew Jackson, David Crockett, or Robert E. Lee, unless it be their flaws and foibles. Yet these men were among my heroes when growing up. I read about them, heard about them, saw movies about them. This was all part of an American boy's life in the 1940s, '50s, and well into the '60s. We didn't hate ourselves then. We were inspired by a Crockett or a Murphy, and we aspired to be like them.

Being reared in the aftermath of World War II meant that, for me, Audie Murphy was the hero of heroes. I had an uncle who served in an outfit under the same command for a time as Murphy's. The uncle could not tell me enough about Murphy, the most decorated American of the war—of any war. I remember my uncle saying—and he was from Superior, Wisconsin, about as far north as one can go in the contiguous forty-eight states, and no particular fan of the Lone Star State—that there is no better, tougher, more courageous fighter on earth than an Irishman from Texas.

Physically, Murphy was only about half a Texan when he enlisted in the army, standing five feet five inches and weighing

110 pounds. But then he had just turned seventeen and would grow two inches and gain twenty-five pounds in the army. Moreover, Murphy had not yet started to shave and looked no more than thirteen or fourteen years old. With auburn hair, blue eyes, freckles, and a baby face, he appeared more cherub than warrior. Nonetheless, "Little Texas," as he was nicknamed in basic training, would rise from private to first lieutenant and be awarded thirty-three medals, including the Medal of Honor, before he turned twenty.

Murphy would seem like the perfect candidate to remain a famous American hero. He was the seventh of twelve children born to a sharecropper and his wife in Hunt County, Texas. He spent most of the years of his youth not inside a classroom but in the fields picking cotton. After the war he wrote a best-selling autobiography and starred in several dozen films, including *To Hell and Back* in 1955, which was Universal's highest-grossing film until 1975. In 1996, the Texas legislature declared his birth date "Audie Murphy Day." Three years later, Texas governor George W. Bush did the same. Yet Murphy is conspicuously absent in school textbooks today and unknown to most students.

While many students today are familiar with the name David Crockett, they cannot say much more about him than he died at the Alamo. Without the Alamo and the many movies made about it, I suspect Crockett also would slip into the mists of history. Since he is with us, though, there has been a concerted effort in both academe and Hollywood to diminish his heroism. Hollywood's latest contribution, *The Alamo*, twists and distorts the very essence of the Tennessee frontiersman nearly beyond recognition. He is full of self-doubt, tortured by his past, and bedeviled by his image. This is not a man who would inspire the loyalty and courage of the men he led, as did the real Crockett.

The movie also suggests that Crockett never really did much of anything and was essentially the creation of early mythmakers. For modern Hollywood, and perhaps for much of modern America, the brave, strong, decisive, iron-willed Crockett must have been the creation of writers and thespians.

While many fictional tales have been spun about Crockett, most of them after his death, the real Crockett did rise from humble beginnings, perform heroic deeds, and die defending his ideals. He may not have killed a bear by the time he was three, but in one season of hunting he did kill more than a hundred bears. On one hunt, his dogs fell into a crevice with a wounded bear. Knife in hand, Crockett leaped in to save his canines and stabbed the bear to death. He fought the Red Stick Creeks in the War of 1812, serving two enlistments and rising to the rank of sergeant. Everyone who hunted with or fought alongside Crockett was awed by his tracking ability, marksmanship, and coolness under fire. Eventually, he became a lieutenant colonel in the Tennessee militia and a three-term congressman.

Although it is not known for certain how Crockett died at the Alamo, revisionist historians argued that he did not fight to the death but was captured and executed. They base this claim on the so-called diary of a Mexican officer, José Enrique de la Peña, who fought at the Alamo. The "diary," however, contains information that was not known until well after the battle. The same revisionists are now admitting that the document could not be a diary and are calling it a memoir in diary form constructed by Peña some years after the battle. Meanwhile, there is considerable evidence that the Peña manuscript is a modern forgery. There is a great irony in all this. The Peña work, a fraud or not, says that Crockett faced death calmly and died courageously.

In *Real Men*, R. Cort Kirkwood tells us the true stories of

Audie Murphy and David Crockett and eight other "Americans to know and admire." They are not all war heroes, but they were all courageous, honorable, and devoted to American ideals—and they all will serve to inspire us and our children. I suspect Americans, especially American parents, are starved for a book that will make them and their children proud of their heritage. The ten men whom Kirkwood vividly describes represent the best America has to offer. May their spirit and legacies never be allowed to pass from the American scene.

—*Roger D. McGrath*
Thousand Oaks, California
January 2005

PREFACE

WHAT IS A real man? Time was, anyone could answer. And any two people would answer similarly, but no longer. Contention conquers consensus.

Today, amid the deafening campaign against traditional Christian and American culture, one cannot hear a straight answer. The exploding din of terms like "chauvinist," and "sexist" and "metrosexual" has drowned out words such as "courage" and "loyalty" and "rectitude." Lying dead in the smoking cultural ruins were the old American heroes who left an unambiguous mark upon the world.

Here, they are resurrected to answer the opening question and to show us what, in these heroes of the past, modern men should admire and emulate.

THE MEASURE OF A MAN

THE MEN in these pages share qualities not only the average man but also the average woman once considered indispensable. They were the attributes every man was expected to possess; a man knew the standard by which he was measured.

It was the standard of a Christian culture, and he knew as well that it wasn't just his church or other men who measured him. He knew a woman wanted a husband worthy not only of her fidelity but also of her gift of unconditional love and of permitting him to father her children and to raise worthy sons and daughters. He knew his children wanted a father of whom they could be proud.

A short list of those qualities included bravery, tenacity, rectitude, integrity, loyalty, faith, chivalry, obedience to God and just authority, and devotion to duty. Undoubtedly, intelligence was another, but it was of less importance, because intelligence is not so much an aspect of character as a congenital tool that, rightly developed, is invaluable. Likewise for physical strength. A smart, strong criminal goes a long way in the world.

More important then were the traits that men once believed symbolized masculinity and that American women once cherished. Indeed, these weren't just qualities men aspired to; they were a part of them, as much a part of them as their legs, arms, and minds. The men in these pages embodied the traditional Christian conception of manhood defined in chivalry. They were honorable and honest, generous to varying degrees to foes, and solicitous and protective of women, children, and animals. They did not brook insults, and they understood that some things are worth dying for. They had guts.

I picked the men profiled in these pages by asking two questions: What kind of men do I want my sons to become? What kind of men do I want my daughters to marry? All these choices embody some manly characteristic I hope to impart to my sons and to teach my daughters to seek in a husband.

In Robert E. Lee, we meet the ideal Christian gentleman, a man of bottomless loyalty and courage who chose certain defeat to defend Virginia from the Yankee usurpers of the old constitutional republic. He was known not only as the handsomest man in the army but also as its finest soldier. So said Gen. Winfield Scott. Lee's rectitude, devotion to duty, and Christian faith were so finely developed, so fully expressed in everything he did, calling him holy would hardly be exaggerating.

In Andrew Jackson, a first-generation American, we meet a duelist and fierce Indian fighter of surpassing valor. Jackson bested the finest marksman in Tennessee with a fatal shot to the stomach, but not before he took a ball in the chest and yet another in the left arm during another shoot-out, which left him so debilitated that when he mounted to ride for Alabama and war against the Red Stick Creeks, they tied him into the saddle. As president, at sixty-eight years old, he felled a would-be assassin with a walking stick.

Meet Lou Gehrig, an athlete who faced creeping, suffocating death with honor, dignity, and courage. And Rocky Versace, a tower of faith and fortitude executed by the Viet Cong. Eddie Rickenbacker was a World War I ace and doer of the impossible. At age fifty-two, he saved six men when his plane crashed at sea. Audie Murphy went to "hell and back" for his country at the Colmar Pocket during World War II. Francis Marion was the feared "Swamp Fox" of the American Revolution, and Davy Crockett was an Indian fighter and hero at the Alamo. Vince Lombardi was a daily communicant admired by millions because of his legendary coaching. Wild Bill Hickok was a fearless gunfighter, lawman, and Indian fighter.

Besides sharing the obvious traits that brought them together in this book, a few of these men suffered the same, potentially damaging psychological and moral handicap. They had father problems. When Lee was eleven, his father died on Cumberland Island off Georgia's coast, having run from debtors. Jackson's father died before he was born. Hickok's father died when James Butler was just fifteen. Rickenbacker's father died when the future aviator was twelve. Murphy's father abandoned his family to the squalor of hardscrabble Texas. Crockett's father was a volcanic, violent drunk who sold his boy into what we would consider slavery. Yet all these boys grew into real men.

In some cases, like Jackson's, a strong mother raised the boy as best she could. In others, like Crockett's, the boy made his own way in the world. Whatever the case, none were failures, and if they had failed, they would not have enjoyed the luxury of an off-the-peg excuse generously furnished by skull doctors and headshrinkers.

What made these men the way they were? Without doubt, genes played a part. Jackson descended from the Celtic Ulster-Scots who settled the Waxhaw country in the Carolinas. Lee devolved from men who fought with William the Conqueror. Marion's blood flowed downstream from the doughty French Huguenots who, after being chased out of France when Louis XIV revoked the Edict of Nantes, settled the malarial low country of South Carolina.

Yet it was more than genes, more than nature. It was nurture. They grew up in a hardscrabble world, some without fathers. In some cases, if they did not work, they did not eat. Crockett had less than a year of school and was on his own at twelve. Murphy reached fifth grade and then went to work to support his family and later earned every combat decoration the country had to offer before he was twenty years old. From childhood, these men knew how they were expected to act. They knew what their mothers and fathers expected. They knew what girlfriends and wives expected. Words like *honor* and *courage* meant something.

So did the word *coward*.

THE DESCENT FROM MANHOOD

BUT THOSE words don't mean much anymore. We don't often hear them, except, for instance, in connection with men having the "courage" to "come out of the closet." The inspiration for this book was positive, as it centers on the things we should love by telling wonderful tales about these men of yore. Yet it was also energized by the things we should despise in modern men, or at least what the culture tells us modern men should be. The culture tells us that men should behave more like women. They do, and that is because the American man in popular culture has been emasculated and feminized.

Hollywood is a main front in the war against traditional Christian culture and its conception of manhood. In fifty short years we have descended from the American man as represented in *The Rifleman* and *Father Knows Best* to the feminized men on *Seinfeld* and *Everybody Loves Raymond*. Once upon a time, television fathers were solid. They loved their wives and children, protected them, and taught their kids right from wrong. *Leave It to Beaver* may have been a little corny, but everyone knew the father, Ward Cleaver, was a good, strong man. He was strict but kind and just. He was faithful to his wife. He always did the right thing. No more. Now, the American man on television is a clown, a helpless husband and father whose wife and children have all the answers and order him around. The slovenly, dull-witted husband and father on *Roseanne* is just one example. Anyone concerned about the menu of options for young boys knows what has happened. Suffice it to say, where Hollywood once gave us *The Rifleman* and *Daniel Boone*, it now offers *Queer Eye for the Straight Guy*.

The late action-movie hero, World War II combat veteran Charles Bronson, made the point. "When you see weakness in a hero, you are doing something to his identity," he told the *Washington Post*. "You take something away from the kids, the next generation, you steal away giving them anything to look up to."

Boys need someone to emulate. Fathers should be their principal example of manhood, but they should read about and see other heroes. Happily, Mel Gibson makes films such as *The Patriot* and *We Were Soldiers,* but the physically or morally weak and confused men in other films numerically overwhelm Gibson's heroes. Gone are the days when the truly masculine and heroic man was the rule, not the exception. The days of *Shane* are over. Now cowboys are the kind depicted in *Brokeback Mountain,* a story about two homosexuals. Bronson was right. American boys have been robbed.

Granted, the weak men we observe in entertainment are fictional characters, but these stereotypical weaklings come from the men and women who create them in scripts and feature them in television programs and advertisements. To the degree that this new American man is held up as an example of the way men are supposed to act, flesh-and-blood men absorb this cultural poison and behave accordingly. The way to become a Christian, the great Christian apologist C. S. Lewis said, is to pretend you're one, to put on the clothes of the Christian to see how they fit. Well, what clothes are men putting on today? Not those of Audie Murphy, the most decorated combat soldier of World War II, or Robert E. Lee, that edifice of manly Christian virtue, or Eddie Rickenbacker, the World War I ace and founder of Eastern Airlines. Rather, our culture says, they should emulate Elton John. Or Alan Alda, the apotheosis of the feminist and feminized man. But sometimes the kind of men American boys and older teenagers want to emulate are even worse. Sports heroes used to be men such as Lou Gehrig. Now we are subjected to the lengthening list of tattooed, pierced thugs in professional sports such as Latrell Sprewell and Mike Tyson.

The disintegration of professional sports aside, the man on the street may well be a "metrosexual." "Male executives find feminine traits pay off in the workplace," a headline in the *Salt Lake Tribune* aptly explained. Metrosexuals "are very secure in their sexuality," ran one report on the phenomenon, and getting a facial or a pedicure "doesn't make them feel any less masculine or any less heterosexual." Metrosexuals are true pioneers, "finding the courage to explore the female domain," another report averred, "without losing their 'status' as real men." Time was, our pioneers were Lewis and Clark and Kit Carson, who traversed and tamed the American wilderness. Now, our men "explore" the "female domain."

Even our armed forces, where masculinity should be and once was exalted, have surrendered. Men in the Pentagon, decorated military heroes who should know better but who fear the wrath of the feminists, send women into combat and ballyhoo the faux derring-do of hundred-pound girls barely out of pigtails and pimple cream, a development that may well be the zenith of the culture war.

A story from Richard Poe appearing at lewrockwell.com in 2003 perfectly illustrates the modern man. Poe tells about the night he was in a Kinko's copy center in New York City when a scuffle broke out at a copy machine. A black man, hurling epithets as he walked out the door, stole a white man's materials.

"Look, he's leaving with my stuff," said the victim, "wringing his hands in frustration."

"Behind the counter," Poe wrote, "were three or four young men in their early twenties, all white, all sporting some combination of bizarre haircuts, earrings, pierced noses, and other countercultural appurtenances. All stared blankly at the customer who was complaining. No one made a move to help," except the "chubby bespectacled" manager, a woman less than five feet tall. Little could the woman do, but she had more courage than the three girly men.

Once upon a time, Poe rightly concluded, young men would have been ashamed to stand by and do nothing because they would fear being labeled a coward. Not anymore.

"As I stood in Kinko's that night," Poe wrote, "it occurred to me that those glassy-eyed young men behind the counter with their earrings and pierced noses did not know this fear. They had probably been taught to fear accusations of 'racism,' 'sexism' and 'homophobia.' But the word coward was not in their vocabulary. They were feminist men." Indeed, they were men for whom the words *honor, courage,* and *coward* meant nothing.

Now read about Roy Lee Hendricks, of Anchorage, Alaska. A few years ago, the *Anchorage Daily News* reported that the octogenarian veteran of the Eighty-second Airborne, which jumped into Normandy on D-day, stopped two teenagers from burglarizing his house. In the fight, he shot himself in the finger, but he beat the daylights out of the two and then drove himself to the hospital. "I never ran in my life, and I don't intend to now," the rough-and-ready Alaskan told the paper. "I'd rather be a dead hero than a live coward."

Men such as Hendricks were taught to fear being labeled a coward. As you read about Audie Murphy and Andrew Jackson, imagine what they would have done if some criminal had tried to rob them.

One might ask how we arrived where we are. It was no single event. It was a concatenation of creeping changes that occurred in our legal system and, more important, in our culture: our literature, our movies, our magazines, our newspapers. It was a metamorphosis because it occurred slowly. But it was also a revolution.

To borrow and modify a few words from Garet Garrett, who chronicled the rise of Franklin Roosevelt's New Deal radicals, there was no day, no hour, no celebration of the event— and yet definitely, the ultimate definition of manhood changed. Some still believe they hold the pass against a revolution that may be coming up the road. But they are gazing in the wrong direction. The revolution is behind them. It went by in the night, singing songs to feminism, diversity, and sensitivity.

MEN ARE RESPONSIBLE

SADLY ENOUGH, men are responsible for this cultural morass, for men were in charge when the foes of masculinity and manhood marched by in the night and sacked our institutions. So men must launch the counterrevolution. They can start by asking what kind of examples they want for their sons and daughters.

Thus this book. It is a book about the kind of men we should admire and hold up as examples of manhood to our sons and, yes, our daughters. Crockett did stay at the Alamo and fight to the last with the men from Texas and old Tennessee. Lee did refuse to betray his native state, despite the knowledge that defeat at the hands of a superior foe was almost certain. Versace did refuse to bend in Communist captivity. These are the men our boys should know, admire, and emulate.

A scene from one of the most morally compelling films ever made, 1963's *Hud*, explains why having good men to admire is crucial to a healthy society. The film is based upon the splendid novel *Horseman, Pass By*, by Larry McMurtry, who, oddly enough, coauthored the screenplay for *Brokeback Mountain*, the ballyhooed film about two homosexual cowboys. Whatever the bizarre worldview or avarice of someone who could write *Brokeback*, *Hud* tells the story of the Bannon family: Hud, his father, Homer, and Hud's nephew, Lon.

The conflict in the film and novel plays out between Hud, a hard-drinking, fighting, unprincipled man with a "barbed wire soul," as the movie posters announced, and Homer, a hard-working rancher of oaken principle. To Lon, Hud is a figure of magnetic masculinity worthy of admiration. In the film's climactic scene, an argument erupts between Hud and Homer. With Lon looking on, Homer upbraids Hud for taking the lad out for a night of drinking.

After Homer tells Hud he is a narcissistic, unscrupulous, grasping cad, Homer warns the boy that beneath Hud's charm lies the soul of an evil man. "You're bein' took in," the wizened sage avers. Lon defends the uncle he admires. "Why pick on Hud, granddad?" the boy asks. "He ain't the only one. Just about everybody around here is like him one way or another."

Replies Homer: "Well, that's no cause for rejoicin', is it? Lonnie, little by little the face of the country changes because of the men we admire."

The country does change, the country has changed. What is a real man? Find out in these ten courageous men we should know and admire.

—*R. Cort Kirkwood*
Penn Laird, Virginia
April 2006

REAL MEN

1

Francis Marion
"The Swamp Fox"

Enthusiastically wedded to the cause of liberty, he
deeply deplored the doleful condition of his beloved
country. The common weal was his sole object; nothing
selfish, nothing mercenary soiled his ermine character.

—*Lighthorse Harry Lee*

THE SWAMP FOX ATTACKED at midnight, his spectral army
emerging from the murky gloom of South Carolina's low-
country bogs along the Black, Santee, and Little Pee Dee
Rivers. Into the Redcoat heart, he struck fear, shock, and awe;
into the hearts of his countrymen, admiration and loyalty.
From August 18, 1780, to September 8, 1781, having commanded troops with Lighthorse Harry Lee and helping
Nathaniel Greene bedevil the British in South Carolina, he established himself as second only to George Washington as a
hero of the Revolution. Such was his legend, partly due to the
inventions of Mason Locke "Parson" Weems, that twenty-
nine cities and seventeen counties bore his name in the twentieth century. And throughout the eighteenth and nineteenth
centuries, he was the eponym for children across the land.

Like so many patriots of the war for independence, Marion
staked his life, fortune, and sacred honor on its outcome. Had
the British won, Marion would have lost more than his Pond

Bluff plantation; most likely, His Majesty's troops would have hanged him for treason. "By nature," wrote biographer Robert D. Bass, "he was gentle, kind and humane," and was, though semiliterate and no highborn magnifico of the plantation gentry, a gentlemen and citizen-soldier whose leadership endeared him to soldier and citizen alike.

EARLY YOUTH AND THE CHEROKEE WAR

FRANCIS MARION was a second-generation American whose French Huguenot grandparents landed in South Carolina in 1685, settling in St. James Parish between the Santee River and Charleston. They fled France when Louis XIV revoked the Edict of Nantes, a law that mandated tolerance for Protestants in the Catholic nation. On the Carolina frontier, the women had to be as hardy as the men, pulling one side of a whipsaw on a downed tree to make a cabin and digging in the ground to farm. As one woman explained, "Since leaving France, we had experienced every kind of affliction, disease, pestilence, famine, poverty and hard labor! I have been for six months together without tasting bread, working the ground like a slave; and I have even passed three or four years without always having it when I wanted it." But survive these resilient colonists did, and they settled and civilized the Carolina wilderness.

Marion sprang from this thick blood in midwinter 1732, and his contemporaries said that he was the runt of the litter. "I have it on good authority," wrote one of his later lieutenants, Peter Horry, "that this great soldier, at his birth, was not larger than a New England lobster, and might easily enough have been put into a quart pot." The youth was afflicted with deformed ankles and knees.

Yet Marion survived the tribulations of colonial life, and at about age fifteen, after hearing romantic stories about ships on the bounty main, he fixed upon a course of life at sea. Thus he sailed as the sixth crewmen aboard a schooner to the West Indies. All went well on the outbound voyage, but on its return, a whale rammed the ship, sundering a plank and opening a seam. The seven men escaped in a lifeboat, and soon after, they found a dog that had abandoned ship with them. After going a week without food or water, the men killed the canine, eating its meat and drinking its blood. The harrowing experience extinguished young Marion's desire to sail the seven seas, and he returned home to work his parents' farm. In 1750, his father Gabriel died, leaving the care of the plantation and his wife, Esther, to Francis.

Young Marion had little education and no formal military training. Like many of the men of his epoch, he began his military exploits by fighting Indians.

In 1756, he and his brother joined the militia. Even as the French and Indian War was ending, the Cherokees were stirring up trouble in South Carolina, and the Marions intended to be there when the arrows flew.

Francis Marion's first trial under fire occurred in 1761, during a campaign against the Cherokees. On a retaliatory raid for an earlier ambush, Lt. Col. James Grant led twelve hundred men up the Santee and Congaree rivers, turning north toward the Cherokee settlement of Echo in North Carolina. When the soldiers reached the scene of the first ambush, where the Indians awaited, Grant ordered Marion and thirty men to remove them. Though Marion was a green soldier, with the composure of a battle-tested warrior, he led his men toward the ambuscade. When the small band was within range, the fierce Cherokees let loose with blood-curdling war whoops and blistering fire, which drove Marion and his men into the protection of the trees. The palefaces fought valiantly, moving ahead one tree at a time. When it was over, twenty-one of Marion's men were dead or wounded, but he prevailed and so, eventually, did Grant.

Fighting for Independence

MARION RETURNED to the quiet life of farming and eventually was elected to the colony's provincial congress. In 1775, when the war for independence began at Lexington and Concord on April 19, Marion was elected captain of the Second Carolina Continentals, and the following year, having been promoted to major, he led his men to defeat the British naval investment of Sullivan's Island. From four hundred yards offshore, eight ships bombarded the fort on the island. The defenders, under Col. William Moultrie, had only fifty-four hundred pounds of gunpowder. Marion commanded the left wing of the fort and its heaviest cannon. He led a party, one story goes, to recover gunpowder from an armed schooner at Stop Gap Creek. The artillery battle raged all day, but the fort's ferocious cannon fire, particularly on the warships *Bristol* and *Experiment,* which wounded Lord Charles Cornwallis, drove the British away at dusk. Legend has it that Marion asked Moultrie if he could fire a parting shot at the British. "Yes," Moultrie cried, "give them a parting kick!" Marion, wrote Robert D. Bass, "touched a match to the powder, and watched the ball rip into the flagship." Peter Horry said that another man fired the round, but either way, wrote Maj. Gen. Charles Lee, "The British sheared off the next morning like earless dogs."

Marion quickly and firmly established himself as a gentlemen soldier and stern commander of his troops. Before the battle at Sullivan's Island, when he learned that one of his lieutenants had lied about visiting a sick father to attend a cockfight, then dissembled again about lingering for another two weeks, Marion uttered an understated yet acerbic rebuke:

"Aye lieutenant, is that you? Well, never mind; there is no harm done. I never missed you."

Marion expected his men to attend church services, and he also enforced rules on hygiene. He ordered hair "cut short" and warned that "any soldier who comes on parade with beards, or hair uncombed, shall be dry-shaved immediately, and have his hair dressed on the parade." Marion, wrote Peter Horry, "wished his officers to be gentlemen. Whenever he saw one of them acting below that character, he would generously attempt the reformation." He expected his men to "behave with Sobriety & Decency."

Having been promoted to lieutenant colonel and then full colonel, Marion distinguished himself in the siege of Savannah, charging the well-defended Spring Hill redoubt. "Sword in hand and shouting encouragement to his men," Bass wrote, Marion crossed a moat toward the British abatis, then "plunged into the ditch. There he stood urging his men forward while the enemy riflemen sprayed death around him."

The patriots did not liberate Savannah, thanks to the ill-conceived decisions of Marion's commanders, but his celestial name and fame were yet to be won. Indeed, his career in the swamps began somewhat inauspiciously. After the action at Savannah, the British moved against Charleston, where Marion, beginning in February, helped to prepare the defenses of the city. In March 1780, Marion attended a dinner party where the men were getting in their cups, toasting liberty and victory over the British. Although he would share a drink or two, he was not drunk. To escape the revelry without embarrassment, he jumped out a window and broke his ankle. In April, as British troops came closer to the city, with Col. Banastre Tarleton killing and burning through the countryside, Marion escaped on a litter into the murky sanctum of the Santee River. Gen. Benjamin Lincoln surrendered the city on May 12,

1780, and six days later, Ban Tarleton crossed the Santee. Thus began the career of the Swamp Fox.

William Dobein James, who as a boy rode with Marion, remembered that Marion wore a coarse crimson jacket and a leather cap that was adorned with a silver crescent and the words "Liberty or Death!" James added that Marion was "rather below the middle stature, lean and swarthy. His body was well set, but his knees and ankles were badly formed, and he still limped upon one leg. He had a countenance remarkably steady; his nose was aquiline, his chin projecting; his forehead large and high, and his eyes black and piercing." Yet even at age forty-eight, Marion's "frame [was] capable of enduring fatigue and every privation."

During his most famous exploits, Marion never led professional soldiers. He led partisans, lowland guerrillas who brought their own weapons and horses into battle, and he shared their deprivations. He was a light eater, reported James, often taking only cold potatoes and water (often mixed with vinegar) once a day. And because his men had no tents, he too slumbered under the canopy of the stars. He was constantly moving, often traveling at dusk to strike somewhere after midnight. "No leader, in ancient or modern times," James wrote, "ever passed rivers with more rapidity. His plans were laid, and his movements conducted, with the most uncommon secrecy. After making a movement, his most confidential officers and men have had to search for him for days together, perhaps without finding him. His scouts, when returning, and at a loss, used a loud and shrill whistle, as a signal; which could be heard in the night to an astonishing distance."

Prowling around the marshlands, Marion burned flatboats and canoes at ferries and along the rivers to deprive the British and their Tory allies of transportation. His men moved like a ghostly army, striking where they wished and tackling their foe

After negotiating a prisoner exchange, Marion invited a British officer to a sparse dinner of sweet potatoes. Later the officer reported, "I have seen an American general and his officers, without pay, and almost without clothes, living on roots and drinking water; and all for LIBERTY! What chance have we against such men!"

in fierce, short battles, then receding into the shadows from whence they struck, leaving the British either speechless or spitting curses. "Fertile in stratagem," Lighthorse Harry Lee reported, "he struck unperceived, and retiring to those hidden retreats selected by himself, in the morasses of Pedee and Black rivers, he placed his corps, not only out of the reach of his foe, but often out of the discovery of his friends."

Marion gained an early victory at the home of Gen. Thomas Sumter, the Carolina "Gamecock." There, he learned from a Loyalist deserter, the British held 150 prisoners. Marion roused his men in the wee hours and rode for Sumter's home, which was festooned in oaks and cedars above Santee Swamp. Peter Horry's patrol happened upon a sentinel, who fired wildly, inspiring Horry's men to rush the house. There they found the British asleep or otherwise lolling, their guns stacked outside. Marion attacked with his main body from the rear. They killed or captured 22 men and freed the prisoners.

Try as they might, the Tories couldn't catch Marion unawares, nor could the British regulars. He was up before dawn and kept patrols moving through his area around the clock. With a force of about fifty, he ambushed and defeated a superior contingent of eighty Loyalists at Blue Savannah.

Fighting in the swamps, Marion braved and bested more than British troops. And yet he himself couldn't swim and indeed feared the water. But he crossed rivers on horseback or clung to the pommel of his saddle, floating beside the steed as it pulled him across. In this manner, Marion crossed the Little Pee Dee River and rode forty-two miles to Black Mingo Swamp. Despite the long trip, his men insisted on attacking immediately, being among their own farms and homes. They defeated a Loyalist force nearly twice their size. At Tearcoat Swamp, Marion struck at midnight and caught Tory troops asleep, capturing eighty horses and muskets along with baggage, food, and ammunition. By November 1780, the British had tired of the rebel's nocturnal brannigans and so unleashed their most feared commander, Ban Tarleton, the man who gave Marion his nom de guerre. "I . . . most sincerely hope you will get at Mr. Marion," Lord Cornwallis wrote to Tarleton. When he learned the location of Marion's camp from two spies, Tarleton, recently recovered from yellow fever, pursued his cunning quarry into the swamps.

On November 7, he landed at the Richardson plantation. Tarleton's plan was to lure Marion to attack by spreading the rumor that his main body had returned to Camden. He also dispatched patrols and demonstrated "tokens of fear," such as leaving campsites with food still cooking over fires. But Mary Richardson sent her son, a Continental officer paroled by the British, to warn the Swamp Fox. Also that night, a prisoner escaped Marion's band. Meeting with Tarleton, he revealed that Richardson's son had enlightened Marion and subverted his attack. Tarleton's dragoons mounted and rode for Marion's men, but the Swamp Fox outfoxed him. Knowing that the fugitive prisoner would squeal, Marion was in the saddle before dawn. He led Tarleton on a seven-hour, twenty-five-mile chase around Jack's Creek and the Pocotaligo and Black rivers. When Tarleton landed at Ox Swamp, he gave up. "Come on, my boys," he yelled. "Let us go back, and we will find the Gamecock [Sumter]. But as for this damned old fox, the Devil himself could not catch him."

The Widow Richardson did not go unpunished. Cantering back to the Santee, Tarleton torched thirty homes. Then returning to Richardson's, he ordered his men to dig up Gen. Richard Richardson, in the grave but six weeks, to "look upon the face of a brave man." He ordered a meal prepared for his trouble, and then he permitted his men to plunder the Richardson home. Finally, he ordered his men to drive the plantation's livestock into the barn, which was stocked with corn, and set the building ablaze. According to Marion, Tarleton then flogged Mary Richardson to force her to reveal Marion's whereabouts.

In March 1781, Marion, by then a brigadier general, trapped Lt. Col. John Watson at the Sampit River, by destroying a bridge so that Watson's troops, twenty of whom were killed, could not cross. Watson, Bass writes, "plunged across the ford, the blood on the wagons tingeing with red the dark waters of the Sampit." That evening, Watson exclaimed, "They will not sleep and fight like gentlemen, but, like savages, are eternally firing and whooping around us at night, and by day waylaying and popping at us from behind every tree!" After this engagement, the ammunition among Marion's men was down to almost nothing.

While Marion's forte was guerrilla warfare, his men stood the test of battle on the open field as well. When Maj. Robert McLeroth sent an officer under a flag of truce to complain that Marion had shot British pickets from ambush, contrary to the rules of war, Marion replied that he would stop shooting pickets when the British stopped burning homes. He added, "If Major McLeroth wishes to see mortal combat between teams of twenty men picked by each side, I will gratify him." McLeroth accepted the challenge, but his troops fled the field.

At Eutaw Springs, Marion's third major engagement after Savannah and Charleston, his men marched into battle with Continentals from North Carolina, Maryland, Virginia, and Delaware. In what may have been the militia's finest hour in the South, they attacked boldly. When it was over, Gen. Nathaniel Greene lauded Marion's men, who discharged seventeen volleys and "fought with a degree of Spirit and firmness that reflects the highest honour upon this class of soldiers." Writing to Baron Friedrich Wilhelm Augustus von Steuben, the Prussian military genius who helped train the Continentals, Greene commented, "Such conduct would grace the soldiers of the great King of Prussia."

When the war ended, Francis Marion preached and practiced reconciliation with the Tory loyalists, those friends and neighbors who did not abandon the Crown but fought against Marion and other patriots. When Jeff Butler, a Tory, sought a proffered amnesty with Marion, the general's men told him they would kill him because he had been particularly cruel to patriots along the Pee Dee. But Marion told his men: "Relying on the pardon offered, the man whom you would destroy has submitted. Both law and honour sanction my resolution to protect him with my life."

Answered the men: "Butler shall be dragged from your tent. To defend such a wretch is an insult to humanity."

Marion did not reply but instead called in his officers and asked them to summon their most trusted followers. "Prepare to give me your assistance," he told the soldiers, "for though I consider the villainy of Butler unparalleled, yet acting under orders as I am, I am bound to defend him. I will do so or perish."

When General Greene suggested that Marion and his men attack the defeated and departing British as they filled their ships with fresh water, the Swamp Fox refused. Drawing more blood was pointless, Marion knew, and taking the moral high ground of a civilized officer and gentlemen, he said, "I would rather send a party to protect them."

A foe of cruelty, Marion fumed when he learned his men executed a prisoner they believed complicit in the murder of his nephew Gabriel. He never ordered them to plunder or burn out Tories, and he refused to obey "Sumter's Law," which permitted officers to pillage the provisions and valuables of citizens to pay and reward their troops. "Of all men who ever drew a sword, Marion was one of the most humane," Horry noted. "He not only prevented cruelty in his own presence, but strictly forbade it in his absence."

Marion became a state senator after the war, and when a bill was introduced to protect officers who partook of the booty owing to Sumter's Law, Hugh F. Rankin noted that Marion demanded his name be withdrawn from the list of those pardoned. "If I have given any occasion for complaint," he said on the senate floor, "I am ready to answer in property and person. If I have wronged any man I am willing to make him restitution. If, in a single instance, in the course of my command, I have done that which I cannot fully justify, Justice requires that I should suffer."

Reported Lighthorse Harry Lee, "During the difficult course of warfare through which he passed, calumny itself never charged him with molesting the rights of person, property or humanity."

Above all, Marion was honorable, and all the traits described herein are the hallmarks of real men worthy of admiration: not only tenacity, valor, and the willingness to sacrifice all, but also the sure knowledge that even the desperate straits foisted upon men by war do not entitle them to do wrong. Thus did this hero refuse to harass the retreating British or mistreat the citizens of this native state, although ordered and permitted to do so.

MARION AND SACRIFICE

FRANCIS MARION was the apotheosis of the citizen-soldier. Militarily, fortune was often fickle. Sometimes he had as many as four hundred men, other times as few as fifty. Once, his men disbanded. But the intrepid commander knew how to improvise. Because of a shortage of ammunition, he turned some infantrymen into cavalry and ordered blacksmiths to hammer whipsaws into broadswords. But Marion never surrendered.

He served his country selflessly, ever enmeshed in brutal warfare amid physically demanding and noxious swamps and marshes. The war not only affected Marion's physical health but also destroyed him financially. When he and his comrades pledged their fortunes, they meant it. Pond Bluff, just a mile off the highway frequently passed by British troops, was destroyed. Marion's house was pillaged and burned, and his cattle and horses scattered or seized. At war's end, the Swamp Fox had to rebuild from nothing.

He was every bit the Cincinnatus that Washington was. Lighthorse Harry Lee, a wealthy and cultured scion of old Virginia, described Marion as a homely, uncultured man, but one whose devotion to duty and common good was single-minded, particularly in securing provender for his men and giving battle to the enemy.

> His visage was not pleasing, and his manners not captivating.
> . . . He possessed a strong mind, improved by its own reflections and observations, not by books or travel. . . . He was sedulous and constant in his attention to the duties of his station, to which every other consideration yielded. . . . The procurement of subsistence for his men, and the continuance of annoyance for his enemy, engrossed his entire mind.
>
> He was virtuous all over; never, even in manner, much less in reality, did he trench upon right. Beloved by his friends, and respected by his enemies, he exhibited a luminous example of the beneficial effects to be produced by an individual who, with only small means at his command, possesses a virtuous heart, a strong head, and a mind directed to the common good.

Marion married Mary Esther Videau in 1786 when he was fifty-four. He left no heirs but prospered on his plantation, where he built a single-story cypress house. "Francis Marion grew old gracefully," Rankin wrote, uttering his final words to his wife on February 27, 1795: "My dear, do not weep for me. I am not afraid to die, for thank God, I can lay my hand upon my heart and say that since I came to man's estate, I have never intentionally done wrong to any man."

The memorial above Marion's grave echoes the words applied to another Frenchman, the Chevalier de Bayard, the Catholic knight sans peur et sans reproche. Marion, the marble headstone reports, "lived without fear and died without reproach."

2

Eddie Rickenbacker

Courage is doing what you're afraid to do.
There can be no courage unless you're scared.

—Eddie Rickenbacker

IT WAS THE SIXTH day, and the fifty-two-year-old leader of the group divided the last of the four oranges. Carefully he cut the orange into eight pieces, which the marooned octet ate greedily. A few consumed the peel and seeds.

Then a strange thing happened, rather a fortuitous omen. A seagull alighted atop the leader's gray fedora. Ever so slowly, the man raised his right hand, inching it skyward toward the bird. With a quick snap of his fingers, he caught the hapless creature and wrung its neck, then defeathered it. Again the group ate hungrily. They used the intestines to catch fish, which they ate raw.

It was 1942, and the group was stranded somewhere in the South Pacific. The man keeping them alive, the leader, was Capt. Eddie Rickenbacker, storied terror of the skies and Medal of Honor recipient in World War I, race-car driver, aviation pioneer, and airline chieftain.

Rickenbacker's story is one of pluck, determination, intelligence, strength of will, character, and unsurprisingly, courage. Planted by his father, these virtues burgeoned in childhood and fully flowered in manhood during his perilous exploits over France against Manfred von Richthofen's Flying Circus, in two plane crashes, and during his stewardship of Eastern Airlines. Rickenbacker's is the tale of a man who never accepted the belief that something was impossible. For him, nothing was.

Early Life and the Great War

EDWARD VERNON RICKENBACKER was born October 8, 1890. His father, William, was a construction contractor and stern disciplinarian who instilled in his boy the beliefs and morals that would serve him later in life.

Then called Reichenbacher (later changed during World War I because it sounded too Germanic), the Swiss boy grew up in Columbus, Ohio. At the age of twelve, tragedy struck hard and fast. His father was killed in a construction accident. Some say William was murdered, but in any event, like many boys of his era, Rickenbacker quit school to help support his family. His first job was at the Federal Glass Factory in Columbus, where he worked 6:00 p.m. to 6:00 a.m., six days a week for $3.50 a week. From there, he took other jobs for $6 and $10 a week and then developed his interest in the novel technology of the day: automobiles. His automobile career began in a repair garage, and after taking a course in mechanical engineering, he landed at the Frayer-Miller automobile company. Charles D. Firestone, the rubber and tire magnate, owned one of the cars, and Rickenbacker was dispatched to the scene when the jalopy broke down outside Columbus.

In the parlance of the day, Rickenbacker was a daredevil.

His love for automobiles grew into a passion for race cars. In 1911, he raced in the first Indianapolis 500 at the famed Brickyard, and three years later, in 1914, he set a world speed record, driving a Blitzen-Benz racer at 134 miles per hour at Daytona Beach, Florida. In 1916, he earned eighty thousand dollars, an unimaginable sum for a man who never made the eighth grade.

The speed demon was in Britain purchasing engines for his racing team when the United States entered World War I. He quickly returned home and tried to persuade the War Department to field a team of pilots who were race-car drivers. The idea didn't get anywhere, but in May 1917 he enlisted in the army, eventually landing in the driver's seat again, this time as a chauffeur for the commander of the American Expeditionary Forces, Gen. John J. Pershing. The job was only a pitstop in the race to his eventual destination. Although Rickenbacker's dream of a team of race-car drivers flying against the Hun never got off the ground, the boy from Columbus did.

The army didn't want Rickenbacker in the air because, at twenty-seven, he was "too old." As well, he was not one of the college-educated, devil-may-care aristocrats who made up the crowd of goggled pilots, white scarves trailing behind them in the wild blue yonder. But he was not deterred. A friend organizing a flight school in France invited Rickenbacker to be its chief engineer, and during his time there, he learned to fly, albeit unconventionally. He showed up unannounced in the classroom to learn and, on the sly, took up planes by himself. His first flight was solo, and with no instructor, he learned to put the plane into a tailspin, which involves shutting off the engine and hurtling toward the ground, then pulling out of the dive at the last minute. He demonstrated his flying prowess over a football game and sent players and fans alike running for cover, so close did he come to the ground. Rickenbacker received his wings.

Shortly after training, he joined the Ninety-fourth Squadron, the legendary Hat-in-the-Ring outfit known for the unique insignia on the side of its Nieuport aircraft. Of course, Rickenbacker was a different kind of pilot, and some of the others didn't like it. The *New York Times* reported in his obituary: "They resented his civilian fame and his undeniable cockiness about it. In addition, he was regarded as uncouth, domineering and profane." Even worse, Rickenbacker brought his engineering and mechanical skills to bear on his own safety. "To top it off," the obituary reported, "he insisted on checking his plane engine before every flight and personally supervised the loading of machine-gun bullets in his ammunition belts, instead of relying on the fortunes of war as gallantry dictated."

Flying against the Germans, or *Fighting the Flying Circus,* as his memoir of World War I is called, Rickenbacker became America's ace of aces, such was his skill, daring, and prowess in the air. He took command of the squadron two months before the war ended. "Just been promoted to command of 94th Squadron," he wrote in his diary. "I shall never ask any pilot to go on a mission that I won't go on. I must work now harder than I did before." That's exactly what Rickenbacker did. His action the next day earned him the Medal of Honor, a story he told in his memoir.

It was September 25, 1918, and the crafty, courageous pilot was heading over Verdun for Etain when he spotted seven German planes heading back to base. Five Fokkers were escorting two photographic observation planes.

Rickenbacker climbed into the sun to get above the German foe, cut off his motor, then dove for the nearest Fokker. "I had him exactly in my sights when I pulled both triggers for a long burst," Rickenbacker wrote. "He made a sudden attempt to pull away, but my bullets were already ripping through his fuselage and he must have been killed instantly. His machine fell wildly away and crashed just south of Etain."

Rickenbacker planned to pull up and away to get above the Huns again, but he changed his plan when he saw that his attack stunned and confused the "Boches," as the Germans were called. Thus did Rickenbacker dive into the formation to attack two LVGs taking photographs.

To down one of these, Rickenbacker performed acrobatics and maneuvers typical of his genius at the joystick. At one point, he saw the enemy's tracer bullets zip past his unprotected face. The dashing hero of the Ninety-fourth was unfazed. He noticed an opening between the two foes that were flying parallel, about fifty yards apart. He dropped into a sideslip and put one of the planes between himself and the other. Leveling his Spad, he began firing. "The nearest Boche," he recalled, "passed directly through my line of fire and just as I ceased firing I had the infinite satisfaction of seeing him gush forth flames. Turning over and over as he fell, the L. V. G.

Eddie Rickenbacker was America's leading ace in World War I with twenty-six victories. He received the Medal of Honor in 1930 for combat action on September 25, 1918, in which he downed two aircraft.

started a blazing path to earth just as the Fokker escort came tearing up to the rescue."

The remaining Fokkers came after Rickenbacker, who wisely disengaged and flew for home. This victory action was typical Rickenbacker. He often attacked a numerically superior enemy, and he frequently took off on solo missions behind enemy lines. He was in France to fight, and fight is what he did.

The next month, Rickenbacker flew into another hornet's nest of the Kaiser's airborne Huns, and he all but vanquished the stinging brood. "Curiously enough," he wrote, "I had gone out over the lines alone that day with a craving desire to get a thrill. I had become 'fed-up' with a continuation of eventless flights." Zooming around behind enemy lines near the Mouse Valley, Rickenbacker spotted the fire from an American observation balloon downed by a German aircraft. When he went to study the flaming spectacle, four Fokkers attacked him from above. Rickenbacker hadn't seen the formation of German fighters that knocked down the American balloon.

Crafty pilot that he was, Rickenbacker knew the Huns ex-

EDWARD V. RICKENBACKER'S CITATION
FOR THE MEDAL OF HONOR

For conspicuous gallantry and intrepidity above and beyond the call of duty in action against the enemy near Billy, France, 25 September 1918. While on a voluntary patrol over the lines, 1st Lt. Rickenbacker attacked 7 enemy planes (5 type Fokker, protecting two type Halberstadt). Disregarding the odds against him, he dived on them and shot down one of the Fokkers out of control. He then attacked one of the Halberstadts and sent it down also.

pected him to dive away, so he took the opposite tactic. He rocketed upward, passing two of the diving Fokkers, but discovered that two more "had remained above on the chance that I might refuse to adopt the plan they had determined upon for me."

Rickenbacker knew he was in for "the fight of [his] life." Indeed, the Fokkers matched him maneuver for maneuver, but Rickenbacker's quick thinking and characteristic audacity did not fail him. He attacked, sending down one plane by aiming directly ahead of him to "compel him either to pass ahead through the path of my bullets or else dip down his nose or fall over his wing. . . . He either preferred the former course or else did not see my bullets." Most likely, Rickenbacker bullets struck the pilot. The other three broke for home, but Rickenbacker's "blood was up," and he gave chase, despite being three miles inside their lines. Rickenbacker's Spad, much faster than the Fokkers, caught one of the three fleeing foes and downed him. By the time it was over, Rickenbacker was just one hundred yards above the ground.

His record at the end of the war? Twenty-six kills in 134 combat missions. He was awarded a record eight Distinguished Service Crosses, and in 1930, one of these was upgraded to America's highest military decoration: the Medal of Honor.

THE HEROICS CONTINUE

AFTER THE war, Rickenbacker graduated to distinguished civilian accomplishments. In 1934, he took over Eastern Airlines for General Motors and turned a $350,000 profit. A few years later, when the government ordered GM to sell the airline, he raised $3.8 million in sixty days to fend off a $3 million bid from a banking syndicate to purchase the airline. He wanted to save it for the "boys and girls who helped build it." He

MOTT'S MILITARY MUSEUM

Tough doesn't begin to describe Rickenbacker. He was recovering from a plane crash when, in October 1942, he went down in the Pacific during an inspection tour. A newspaper dubbed him the "Great Indestructible."

refused to follow the conventional belief that an airline could exist only with government subsidies. Rickenbacker never took a dime of government money, and he captained the airline at a profit until 1960, when he retired as chairman. His original salary of $50,000 annually never increased. During this period, he bought and sold the Indianapolis Speedway. But he was to suffer two more harrowing adventures in the years well beyond the blossom of youth.

The first occurred in February 1941, when he was aboard an Eastern Airlines plane that flew into a mountain outside Atlanta, Georgia. As the *New York Times* recorded it, Rickenbacker was "pinned to the body of a dead steward" and suffered a shattered hip, six broken ribs, a broken leg, and a torn eyelid. Yet he was conscious for nine hours until he landed in the hospital. Perhaps inevitably, given his character, Rickenbacker stepped into command of the plane and survivors during the long interlude and sent the walking wounded for help.

When rescuers came, wrote W. L. White in the introduction to Rickenbacker's *Seven Came Home,* "Eddie's great voice of command came booming out from under the debris, only slightly muffled by the wreckage and the dead man who lay on top of him. 'Please be calm,' he told the rescuers, 'Please don't light any matches.'"

Rickenbacker was still recovering from this crash when Secretary of War Henry Stimson sent him on a secret mission to inspect U.S. air bases around the world. The travel took Rickenbacker first to Europe, after which he returned to leave for the Pacific. Rickenbacker's second ordeal in less than a year began at 1:30 a.m. on October 21, 1942, when he and seven other men took off in a Flying Fortress for "Island X," as he calls it in *Seven Came Home,* eighteen hundred miles across the Pacific Ocean.

Flying a plane with poor navigational equipment, the pilot missed the island. While searching for it, he ran out of gas, which forced him to ditch at sea. Eight passengers survived the crash, and although all were military, including some of high rank, Rickenbacker, accoutered in a business suit and gray fedora, took command.

Planning ahead was a Rickenbacker trademark. During World War I, as commander of the Ninety-fourth Squadron, he insisted that planes be gassed up and ready to go, with a full complement of ammunition, at a moment's notice. His foresight served the survivors well in the Pacific, given the truth of what crewman told him as the plane was going down: "Rick, I hope you like the sea. I think we're going to spend a long time on it." They gathered everything they would need, including four of Rickenbacker's handkerchiefs, and stowed the supplies near the hatch where they would leave the plane when it crashed into the sea, which quickly rushed in upon impact. One man was severely injured in the crash; another cut his fingers to the bone trying to unknot a line to Rickenbacker's raft. Three rafts put to sea from the downed plane, with three men each in two and two men in another.

The sun became the crew's foe. It blistered them head to toe, leaving raw, red skin then scalded by the lapping, briny waves. The rafts were not big enough for the men, and when they turned or moved at night, they often scraped their painful skin against one another. Night offered the opposite problem of the day. Cold mist chilled them to the bone. Eventually, the men settled into a routine of prayers, Bible readings, and talking about the stars, and they sent up flares a few times a day to attract any rescuers scouting the area. One crewman brought a gun, but it rusted before he could use it to shoot a gull.

By the eighth day they had run out of food. The oranges had gone two days earlier, and the men were dying of thirst. That's when the gull landed on Rickenbacker's head. He killed the bird, then used the remains to bring in fish. Next day, they paddled into a Pacific squall to get rainwater. The men used their clothes to absorb the rain, then wrung them out, collecting the desperately needed fresh water in buckets and other storage containers. Rickenbacker collected rainwater and transferred it by mouth into a Mae West life jacket.

On the thirteenth morning, one of the men died, and his mates mournfully cut him adrift into the Pacific. For another eight days, they collected rainwater, sharing it equally. They tried killing and eating shark, but gagged on the foul-tasting meat. Meanwhile, sharks bumped their rafts. One pack of sharks attacked a school of mackerel near the rafts; the prey "shot out of the water like star shells." Two of them landed in the life rafts, providing food for two days. One shark inadvertently slapped a crewman's face, and another tore a hole in one of the rafts. Eventually, the group decided the three rafts should separate and seek help on their own. Rickenbacker argued against it, but he eventually gave in.

"It does us no dishonor," he wrote, "to say we were all becoming a little unhinged. Wrathful and profane words were exchanged over nothing at all." The men condemned the Lord because they expected to be rescued immediately, and Rickenbacker went to work on his marooned mates mentally. He tried to assure the men that the longer they were at sea, the more they would appreciate their rescue, and failing that, he simply got mean. He admitted brutalizing the men verbally and exploiting a greater fear than death: the fear of being called a coward by a man such as Rickenbacker. He had to "jar those whose chins sagged too far down on their chests," he recalled, which invited one man to yell across the Pacific's lapping waves, "You are the meanest, most cantankerous so-and-so that ever lived."

Rickenbacker and six members of his crew were adrift in these two liferafts for three weeks in the Pacific.

Rickenbacker was an industrial renaissance man. With little formal education, he became the head of Eastern Airlines—which ran a profit without government subsidies—and owned the Indianapolis Speedway.

Rickenbacker knew what he was doing. He understood men. He understood what motivates them. "Several of the boys," he wrote, "confessed that they once swore an oath to live for the sheer pleasure of burying me at sea." And live they did. On the twenty-second day, deliverance came for Rickenbacker and the six other survivors. He had lost some fifty pounds, but the first-generation American, born of hardy Swiss stock, was little worse for the wear. On his return, the photo in the *Boston Globe* was captioned, "The Great Indestructible."

AMERICAN MAN OF YORE

RICKENBACKER DID not know the meaning of the words *defeat* or *surrender*. *Impossible* was another unfamiliar word. When he gave employees a task they considered impossible, he did it himself to prove it wasn't.

Rickenbacker died on July 27, 1973. He was a giant who straddled the American stage, a man endowed with that ineffable something that put him ahead and beyond other men. Yet some things can be described. He was a man of defiant determination, a will to succeed; he rejected limitations. Yet he was also man of thrift, stern morals, high intellect, and assiduous work. He was physically courageous and in some sense reckless, a typical fighter pilot. Said Gen. Jimmy Doolittle, hero of the 1942 bombing raid on Tokyo in World War II, "Eddie exemplifies those qualities which made America great: courage, integrity, intelligence, humanity, spirituality and patriotism; together with the ability to plan ahead and then a willingness to work hard—and sacrifice—to achieve and prevail."

He was the American man of yore. He was the kind of man who, like others in these pages, little boys used to read about in short biographies. Learning of men such as Rickenbacker is what young boys need. He rose from nothing, mastered the new sport of auto racing, taught himself to fly the rickety planes of the Great War, repeatedly plunged headlong into aerial combat and built a profitable airline from virtually nothing.

He was an inspiration, the kind of example our nation, particularly our sons, so desperately needs.

3

Vince Lombardi

Coach Lombardi showed me that by working hard and
using my mind, I could overcome my weakness to the
point where I could be one of the best.

—*Bart Starr*

Winning isn't everything, it's the only thing."

Thus ran one of the most famous aphorisms from one of
the most famous football coaches in the annals of athletics,
Vince Lombardi. But Lombardi did not originate the words,
which first surfaced in the John Wayne film *Trouble Along the
Way,* and if Lombardi ever repeated it, he never believed the
literal meaning. Still, the words have been forever linked with
him. By the time cancer felled him in 1970, he was one of the
most beloved men in the country, worshipped by players and
fans alike. At games, you could see "Lombardi for President"
signs. More than three thousand mourners attended his funeral at St. Patrick's Cathedral in Manhattan. Others hated
him and what they viewed as his overbearing arrogance and
intolerance. Yet regardless of what anyone thought, he won.
And his teams won. For that, his players respected him.

He was born June 11, 1913, and lived the prime of his life,

as biographer David Maraniss titled his biography, "when pride still mattered." Yet Lombardi's wasn't sinful pride; it wasn't hubris. His was the manly pride in doing one's best all the time, always trying to win. Not incidentally, for Lombardi, doing one's best in one chosen's field also gave glory to God. A pious Catholic who considered the priesthood, Lombardi understood human behavior and how to motivate men. He forged bonds among them with discipline and hard work, making them a cohesive unit aiming toward one goal: winning football games.

Throughout his career, from coaching high-school players to West Point and to the Green Bay Packers, he molded men, built teams, and proclaimed the gospel of hard work, achievement, personal excellence, and victory.

The Coach

Perhaps Lombardi's greatest skill lay in his ability to motivate men. He demanded practice, obedience to rules, order, and discipline. In military terms, he was a drill instructor, and a tough one at that. Yet he also used simple psychology to inspire the men, or boys early in his career, under his charge.

After playing at Fordham as one of the "Seven Blocks of Granite," in 1939, Lombardi took over as football coach at St. Cecilia's High School in Englewood, New Jersey. He worked the boys as hard as he worked himself. The coach also taught physics, chemistry, and Latin, an eclectic, erudite mix of subjects for a man whose principle love was sport. He was something of a Renaissance man.

Lombardi's tactics with high-school boys included giving them the confidence and strength to hit hard, but not unfairly, by practicing on him. "Hit me! Hit me!" he would command them. Once, when a halfback uncorked a "vicious" elbow to Lombardi's chin, Maraniss reported, "The coach smiled and thundered, 'That's the way to do it!'" On another occasion, he torqued his team into a fury when they were about to tackle a much tougher opponent. In preparing for the game against Brooklyn Prep, Lombardi assembled his charges in the locker room and read a series of "nasty letters and telegrams that he said had been sent from Brooklyn." Fired into a healthy rage, the team won. The players never knew Lombardi concocted the scurrilous mail. One player from St. Cecilia remembered that Lombardi "would knock you down, then build you up. He understood human behavior better than any person I've ever met."

Vince Lombardi's gargantuan persona made him the most beloved, feared, and respected coach of all time. Here he discusses a play with quarterback Bart Starr (15) in the Packers 33–14 victory over the Oakland Raiders at Super Bowl II at the Orange Bowl in Miami, Florida.

VERNON BIEVER/WIREIMAGE.COM

Lombardi knew how to motivate men by speaking about excellence, perseverance, and discipline as the keys to winning. One of the beneficiaries was Packers linebacker Ray Nitschke, who stands behind the coach above.

Lombardi went from St. Cecilia's to coach at Fordham and then West Point, where he plotted football strategy with Gen. Douglas MacArthur. Next, he landed with the New York Giants, where he was the offensive coordinator, and Tom Landry was his defensive counterpart. From New York, he went to Green Bay, Wisconsin, where he took over a struggling, pathetic team named the Packers, a name that will forever be connected to Lombardi.

From the beginning, Lombardi stressed arduous practice. His emotional investment in his team was legendary, and he was given to shouting, cursing, and berating his players. Some questioned his tactics; not all men respond to them. Yet here Lombardi was dealing with men, not children; they could have left at any time. Few did. If Lombardi was anything, he was decent and fair. And he was just. He did not favor one player over another. On one occasion, Maraniss reported, he went full bore after Em Tunnell, the best running back on the team, and twice ordered him off the field to run punishment laps. "But Vincent and Em were the only ones wise to the Old Man's trick. Lombardi was using Em, his old friend from the Giants, to demonstrate to the others that even a veteran all-star was not above discipline on his team."

Lombardi knew his discipline should never demoralize the team, which brings up Max McGee, who paid many a fine for breaking the rules. Knowing how much Lombardi liked McGee, the rest of the players would more easily fall into line. And Lombardi used the money he took from players in fines for a postseason party. And one year, McGee got his money back.

Understanding that men need to unwind, he did not carry petty rules to extremes. Lombardi imposed a rule that his players were not to stand at the hotel bar and drink; tables were fine, but no hanging at the bar. Players who violated the rules were fined. Yet whenever he was returning to a hotel from dinner, he would send one of his coaches ahead to the hotel bar to warn the players that he was coming and to get away from the bar. He didn't want to fine them.

Lombardi expected his players to behave and dress like gentlemen and professionals; they wore shirts and ties when they traveled. Once, Maraniss wrote, the New York Jets and Packers landed at the San Francisco airport at the same time. Most of the Jets players were wearing faded T-shirts. Lombardi took one look at his slovenly opponents, pointed them out to his players, and said, "Take a look at them! We don't look like that. That's not us. We're professionals."

If you want the measure of a man, ask those who knew him what they thought of him. Some of the remarks are amusing, revealing the kind of discipline he inspired, but others reveal his true character. Not least among his qualities was the authority he commanded, which led Forrest Gregg to quip, "When Lombardi said 'sit down,' we didn't look for a chair." Some men did not fear Lombardi as much as they feared not making the team. That, of course, was because "he made you a believer," said Willie Davis. Lombardi knew the football business, and he knew what had to be done to beat another team. Invariably, the players found, he was right. Like all good coaches, Lombardi's discipline inspired his men to exceed their own expectations. "He pushed you to the end of your endurance and then beyond it," Henry Jordan said. "And if there was reserve there, well he found that too." Lombardi's relentless drive for perfection in his teams ended in their nonpareil excellence.

Almost uniformly, the Packers loved him, and that is because he loved them. "He loved his players and his teams," one player remembered, Maraniss reported, and "gave sermons about the meaning of love." One player remembered his words:

> Anybody can love something that is beautiful or smart or agile. You will never know love until you can love something that isn't beautiful, isn't bright, isn't glamorous. It takes a special person to love something unattractive, something unknown. That is the test of love. Everybody can love someone's strengths and somebody's good looks. But can you accept someone for his inabilities?

In Green Bay, Lombardi's work paid off. His teams went 98–30–4, with six division titles and five NFL championships, and they claimed the first two Super Bowls.

VERNON BIEVER/WIREIMAGE.COM

Lombardi remolded the Green Bay Packers through discipline and hard work. He turned them into on of the best teams in the NFL throughout the 1960s. He was harsh but fair, and most of his players loved him.

A DEVOUT CATHOLIC

MORE IMPORTANT than his football prowess, however, was Lombardi's devotion to God. He was an ardent Catholic who attended daily mass. He prayed before he went to work, particularly to St. Anthony and St. Jude, and carried a black, wooden rosary. Such was Lombardi's devotion to the rosary that he equipped his car, Maraniss wrote, with a snap-on, fluorescent rosary for the steering wheel so he could pray while driving at night.

Lombardi was cursed with a terrible temper and impatience, but he understood these were not only failings but also traits that could be turned to good use, particularly in motivating players. Thus, "his daily prayers," Maraniss noted, "were an effort to balance the tension between his will to succeed and his desire to do good." Unlike so many of us today,

Lombardi understood he was a sinner. At least in his early years, he went to confession several times a week. The priest with whom he worked at St. Cecilia's remembered, "We'd be sitting there talking about something and all of a sudden Vinnie would say, 'Tim, I want to go to confession.' So I'd take his confession right there from my desk and when he was done we'd start right back into the conversation we had going before."

Lombardi's urge toward discipline and order, as well as repetition with the goal of perfection, flowed logically from the Jesuit education he had received at Fordham University.

Vince Lombardi not only was a master of motivating men but also a master of articulating his philosophy. Here are a few of his pithy observations of men, winning, and life:

The quality of a person's life is in direct proportion to their commitment to excellence.

Mental toughness is many things and rather difficult to explain. Its qualities are sacrifice and self-denial. Also, most importantly, it is combined with a perfectly disciplined will that refuses to give in. It's a state of mind—you could call it character in action.

There's only one way to succeed in anything, and that is to give it everything. I do, and I demand that my players do.

If you aren't fired with enthusiasm, you'll be fired with enthusiasm.

Leaders are made, they are not born. They are made by hard effort, which is the price which all of us must pay to achieve any goal that is worthwhile.

"We have God-given talents and are expected to use them to our fullest whenever we play," he said. Lombardi believed men must always strive for perfection in everything to glorify God: *ad majorem Dei gloriam.*

For all of Lombardi's bravado and bluster, he was a just man whose players knew that an unswerving standard of fairness lay beneath his outward mien. He was a humble man who expected obedience not only from his players and coaches but also from himself, meaning obedience to his church and God. He was a man of strict conscience, and he demanded nothing more of others than he demanded of himself.

> Once you learn to quit, it becomes a habit.
>
> Winning is not a sometime thing; it's an all-time thing. You don't win once in a while, you don't do things right once in a while, you do them right all the time. Winning is a habit. Unfortunately, so is losing.
>
> It's easy to have faith in yourself and have discipline when you're a winner, when you're number one. What you've got to have is faith and discipline when you're not yet a winner.
>
> I firmly believe that any man's finest hour, the greatest fulfillment of all that he holds dear, is the moment when he has worked his heart out in a good cause and lies exhausted on the field of battle—victorious.
>
> Winning isn't everything—but wanting to win is.
>
> In great attempts, it is glorious even to fail.

An Inspiration

LOMBARDI WAS an inspiration for millions of Americans. Thoughtful and intelligent, his intellectual prowess was exceeded only by his ambition to win. In many of his most famous quotes, you hear the words of one driven not merely to victory but to unalloyed excellence, victory regardless. Lombardi hated losing, but he preferred losing a well-played, hard-fought game to winning a lackluster, poorly played game.

In his words you hear timeless truths translated into the unique patois of the football coach. He talked about character, toughness, sacrifice, teamwork, excellence, and winning. Hearing Lombardi, you nod your head and mutter, "Yeah, that's right."

"Get a haircut!" he once roared to a young teenager assisting the team. One cannot imagine what Lombardi would do with a "metrosexual" cornerback, a pony-tailed linebacker, a fullback wearing two earrings, or a ludicrous character such as Dennis Rodman. He would look at them and say what he said when he saw the Jets emerge from their plane: "That's not us." When Lombardi said "that's not us," he meant that his team, his men, were different. They were cut from a different bolt of cloth, and he expected them to comport and accouter themselves appropriately, that is, like real men. And that's what made Lombardi who he was. It wasn't just winning, it was his character and what he expected of the men he coached. It was his demand for excellence. Imagine what his reaction would be if told his boys would have to play with girls or that a woman would be the place kicker for West Point. Lombardi could never coach today, professionally or at a high school or college. But that truth isn't as much an observation about Lombardi as on the modern American athlete in particular and modern American man in general. Gen. George

S. Patton could not command troops in today's army. Wild Bill Hickok could not be a modern lawman. Andrew Jackson could not be elected president.

The question is whether that says something about them or something about us.

4

Rocky Versace

They couldn't break him, they couldn't even bend him.

—*Lt. Col. Nick Rowe*

HE WAS TALL, DARK, and handsome, athletically built, and flashed a wide, merry grin. Looking at his picture, you can imagine him in high school, striding down the hall in a sport coat and tie with an easy gait and a ready smile. He could have been any kid in the 1950s, but he wasn't. He was Humbert Roque "Rocky" Versace, West Pointer, Army Ranger, and recipient of the Medal of Honor for courage in captivity in Vietnam.

Like other stories in this book, his is the story of surpassing fortitude. But Versace's biography goes beyond an impulsive act of bravery on the battlefield, beyond a fierce firefight for thirty minutes or an hour or even a day. Versace's story is one of tenacious endurance in captivity for more than two years and unyielding courage in the face of physical deprivation, starvation, and unrelenting, unspeakable mental and physical cruelty. Versace's story, perhaps the least well-known in this book, is one of Christian faith, the kind of steadfast bravery we read about in the lives of the saints who, like Versace, were tortured unmercifully before death.

Versace was only recently recognized for his surpassing valor, but even the accolades to which he is justly entitled won't make his name a household word, although it should be. Versace's faith and bravery were of the kind that ensured the survival of Christianity, the exploration of the new world, and the founding of the republic. In Versace, we find not just courage but the distilled essence of Christian fortitude.

"Atrocious" Resolve

Humbert Roque Versace was born July 2, 1937, into a family of stout Roman Catholic faith. His father was a career army man who, like all army men, moved frequently from post to post. Eventually, the family landed in Alexandria, Virginia, and Rocky went to Gonzaga College High School, a Jesuit institution on North Capitol Street in Washington, D.C. A daily communicant, Versace followed his father's path to the U.S. Military Academy at West Point.

Versace's family, friends, and acquaintances remember one outstanding quality. He never gave in, either in intellectual or physical combat, whether in sports or on the battlefield. One newspaper account describes his tenacity. On his way to Vietnam, he stopped in Hawaii to see his brother and challenged him to one-on-one in basketball. They played for four and a half hours until Rocky won. "I told him he'd never beat me. But he wouldn't let me go until he'd won," Steve Versace told the reporter. "That was Rock." As well, Versace was always one to argue, which served him well when butting heads not only with the Jesuits but also with the army officers at West Point. He was under strict military discipline, so he was no stranger to the punishment drill, yet this determined, muley cadet served the priest at Mass every day.

"If he thought he was right," Steve Versace said, "he was a

A 1959 graduate of the U.S. Military Academy at West Point, Rocky Versace (first row, sitting at far right) served two tours in Vietnam before he was captured, tortured, and executed.

pain in the neck. If he knew he was right, he was absolutely atrocious." Absolutely atrocious he would have to be to survive what fate had in store in 1963.

COMBAT AND CAPTIVITY

GRADUATED AS an armor officer in 1959, Versace served briefly in the Third Infantry's "Old Guard" then volunteered for duty in Vietnam. After language training in French and Vietnamese, he landed there in 1961 as an Army Ranger.

The West Pointer survived his first tour of duty unscathed and volunteered for a second. It was nearly over when he volunteered to accompany the special forces on an assignment with the Vietnamese unit to which he was attached as an

VERSACE FAMILY PHOTOGRAPH

Versace was "the finest example of an officer I have known," one of his comrades said. The last his men heard from him, he was singing "God Bless America" at the top of his lungs before he was executed.

adviser. Their mission: attack a unit of Viet Cong that had established a base at Le Coeur, a hamlet in Viet Cong territory at the edge of the U Minh Forest in the Mekong Delta. Though the Americans got the drop on the Viet Cong, who fled under the fierce attack as anticipated, the enemy fled in the wrong direction, away from another U.S. detachment set up to intercept them. Eventually, the Viet Cong regrouped and turned the tables on the Americans. Using automatic weapons and mortar fire, the Viet Cong quickly zeroed in on the U.S. position.

The black-clad guerrillas bested the Americans, whom they forced to retreat. The late Lt. Col. Nick Rowe, who told Versace's story in detail, saw the ranger go down with three shots into his left leg and back from a Browning automatic rifle. A grenade would have killed Versace had he not fallen as it exploded; Rowe took some of the impact in the face. Still, Rowe moved to help his fallen comrade and bandage his leg, which was spurting blood like a "fire hydrant." The Viet Cong captured the two men and others, stripping them of weapons and shoes, then marching them back to their makeshift prison camp in the dense jungle. It was October 29, 1963.

Immediately, Versace, the senior officer, took command of the POWs. The Viet Cong clapped them in leg irons and imprisoned them in cages six feet long, two feet wide, and three feet high, deep in the mangroves. The communist guerrillas kept the men on a starvation diet of rice, salt, and water. Often they were stripped and left naked against the elements. The mosquitoes were so thick, fellow POW Dan Pitzer remembered, they resembled black socks on his ankles. Rowe explained the savage torture to which Versace was subjected:

> He was kept in irons, flat on his back, it was dark and hot [from thatch on the roof and outside bamboo walls], and they only let him out to use that latrine and to eat. What they were trying to do was to break him. They even offered better food and they would let him out if he would cooperate, but he would not.

Ever disputatious, Versace was a problem for the Viet Cong. He demanded that he and his men be treated humanely, in accordance with the Geneva Convention that governs the conduct of war and treatment of prisoners. Their answer? Torture. When Versace refused to give more information than name, rank, serial number, and date of birth, they twisted his wounded leg. In addition to seeking information about the American forces arrayed against them, the Viet Cong cadres subjected the men to "re-education" sessions about the history of Vietnam and the virtues of Communism, hoping to break their will and persuade them to denounce the United States. Versace refused. During the indoctrination sessions, he argued with his captors in French and Vietnamese, rebutting their ideological arguments and cursing at them. On one occasion, the Viet Cong needed two guards to force Versace to go. "You can make me come to this class," Versace told them, "but I am an officer in the United States Army. You can make me listen, you can force me to sit here, but I don't believe a word of what you are saying."

Versace "was engaging all comers," Rowe wrote of these classes. One of Versace's tormentors would "completely lose his composure, yelling 'No! No! No!' when Rocky maneuvered him into a contradiction. . . . After a while, the cadre stayed primarily with French and English to prevent the guards from understanding Rocky's counterarguments which might have adversely influenced the indoctrinations they were receiving."

"He told them to go to hell in Vietnamese, French, and English," Pitzer recalled. "He got a lot of pressure and torture, but he held his path. As a West Point grad, it was Duty, Honor, Country. There was no other way." Because of his belligerence, the Viet Cong focused their attention on breaking him, which lightened the burden and misery of captivity on the other men.

Versace sang familiar songs to his men to maintain their esprit de corps and morale, and he left notes for them in the common latrine. "Unyielding, he steadfastly continued to berate the guards for their inhuman treatment," one official account reports. "The communist guards simply elected harsher treatment by placing him in an isolation box, to put him out of earshot and to keep him away from the other US POWs for the remainder of his stay in camp. However CPT Versace continued to leave notes in the latrine for his fellow inmates, and continued to sing even louder."

Of course, Versace tried escaping. Three weeks after he was captured, the official record reports:

CPT Versace took advantage of the first opportunity to escape when he attempted to drag himself on his hands and knees out of the camp through dense swamp and forbidding vegetation to freedom. Crawling at a very slow pace, the guards quickly discovered him outside the camp and recaptured him. After

VERSACE FAMILY PHOTOGRAPH

Versace was to leave Vietnam for the Maryknoll seminary just two weeks after the Communists captured him. He hoped to return to Vietnam as a missionary priest and to help underprivileged children.

recapture CPT Versace was returned to leg irons and his wounds were left untreated. He was placed on a starvation diet of rice and salt.

Versace made three more attempts, but he was recaptured then manacled, gagged, and again placed on reduced rations.

Because of his stubborn resistance not only to torture but also to the blandishments of better food and easier captivity, the Viet Cong labeled him a "reactionary" and "uncooperative." They subjected him to more torture as they dragged him through villages, yoked with a rope around his neck like a beast of burden, parading him in front of villagers to show the broken American. But the Vietnamese and even the Viet Cong never saw a broken man. The Vietnamese said the worse he appeared physically, the more he smiled and talked about God and America. Farmers and even guards testified to Versace's unwavering fortitude and faith in God and country.

For nearly two years, Versace never wavered from the code of conduct. He never gave an inch. Versace was "the finest example of an officer I have known," Pitzer said. "To him it was a matter of liberty or death. . . . Once, Rocky told our captors that as long as he was true to God and true to himself, what was waiting for him after this life was far better than anything that could happen now. So he told them that they might as well kill him then and there if the price of his life was getting more from him than name, rank, and serial number."

The last time Rowe saw Versace, his hair had grown white and his skin yellow from jaundice. He was a shadow of the two-hundred-pound warrior Rowe had known. The last anyone heard of him, he was singing "God Bless America" at the "top of his lungs" from his isolation box. On September 29, 1965, retaliating for the execution of two Viet Cong by the South Vietnamese, the Viet Cong executed Rocky Versace.

Versace (below, left) often assisted priests during celebrations of the Mass. When he received his combat infantry badge from his father (below, right), his expression was that of a man with a mission who radiated pride in the task at hand.

THE MEDAL OF HONOR

LT. COL. NICK ROWE returned from Vietnam with a singular mission: to ensure Versace was remembered. Rowe, who escaped and survived the war only to be assassinated by Philippine Communists in the 1980s, wrote about Versace in his book *Five Years to Freedom*. Rowe's account, as well as that of other prisoners, contains everything we know of Versace's heroism in the jungles of Vietnam, and they were duly recorded in the package submitted for Versace's Medal of Honor.

Rowe's esteem was boundless, and he was determined that Versace would receive the nation's highest decoration for bravery. He met with President Richard Nixon and told him Versace's story. When he finished, the president, tears in his eyes, hugged Rowe. "Get that man the Medal of Honor," Nixon told a military aide. Somehow, it did not happen, and the army gave Versace a Silver Star. Eventually, a group called the Friends of Rocky Versace renewed the crusade for the medal. On July 8, 2002, they succeeded, with President George W. Bush presenting the medal in an emotional ceremony at the White House. But the group wasn't finished. In a lasting tribute to this fine man, they erected a monument in Alexandria, Virginia, at the city's Vietnam War memorial. The bronze effigy depicts the hero with two children. So do many of the pictures Versace sent home from Vietnam. The children are smiling, and so, of course, is Rocky.

Versace is depicted with children for good reason. He fervently wished to devote his life to them. When he was captured, the Gonzaga boy was just two weeks away from leaving Vietnam and entering seminary; he planned to become a Maryknoll missionary. He wanted nothing more than to become a priest, and after that, his ambition was to return to Vietnam to help orphans.

HUMBERT R. "ROCKY" VERSACE'S CITATION
FOR THE MEDAL OF HONOR

Captain Humbert R. Versace distinguished himself by extraordinary heroism during the period of 29 October 1963 to 26 September 1965, while serving as S-2 Advisor, Military Assistance Advisory Group, Detachment 52, Ca Mau, Republic of Vietnam. While accompanying a Civilian Irregular Defense Group patrol engaged in combat operations in Thoi Binh District, An Xuyen Province, Captain Versace and the patrol came under sudden and intense mortar, automatic weapons, and small arms fire from elements of a heavily armed enemy battalion. As the battle raged, Captain Versace, although severely wounded in the knee and back by hostile fire, fought valiantly and continued to engage enemy targets. Weakened by his wounds and fatigued by the fierce firefight, Captain Versace stubbornly resisted capture by the overpowering Viet Cong force with the last full measure of his strength and ammunition. Taken prisoner by the Viet Cong, he exemplified the tenets of the Code of Conduct from the time he entered into Prisoner of War status. Captain Versace assumed command of his fellow American soldiers, scorned the enemy's exhaustive interrogation and indoctrination efforts, and made three unsuccessful attempts to escape, despite his weakened condition which was brought about by his wounds and the extreme privation and hardships he was forced to endure. During his captivity, Captain Versace was segregated in an isolated prisoner of war cage, manacled in irons for prolonged periods of time, and placed on extremely reduced ration. The enemy was unable to break his indomitable will, his faith in God, and his trust in the United States of America. Captain Versace, an American fighting man who epitomized the principles of his country and the Code of Conduct, was executed by the Viet Cong on 26 September 1965. Captain Versace's gallant actions in close contact with an enemy force and unyielding courage and bravery while a prisoner of war are in the highest traditions of the military service and reflect the utmost credit upon himself and the United States Army.

Thus did Versace's service to the United States segue into service to God, much like that of Ignatius Loyola, the soldier-turned-priest who founded the Society of Jesus, or Jesuits, who had trained Versace so well. Rocky loved God and country. He died for both, a soldier fighting against atheist Communism. In a sense, Versace was a martyr, not only for his country but also for his faith, a truth best demonstrated by what he was singing when he was last known alive: "God Bless America."

As young people have forgotten Audie Murphy and the other men in these pages, they have never heard the story of Rocky Versace. In 1972, Rowe said, "How many people in America today know or remember Rocky Versace? How many people even in the Army remember him? They've forgotten Rocky Versace. And it is important that he be remembered. We don't have that many Rocky Versaces and we need them. It is a tragedy that he is virtually forgotten."

What a statement Rowe makes: we don't have that many Rocky Versaces. No, we don't. We need more of them, but we won't get them if we forget them. Versace's story is not only one of inconceivable physical courage but also one of plenary sacrifice and true filial love. Perhaps more than any of the other men in these pages, Versace is a model for men in that lone regard. He gave everything he had, not for himself, but for his fellow prisoners. He didn't worry about himself; he worried about his comrades. The man from West Point followed the teaching of the Man from Galilee, to whom he was ready to devote his life: "Greater love has no man than this, that he lay down his life for his friends" (John 15:13).

Rocky Versace must be remembered and honored forever, perhaps for one reason more than any other, as Rowe explained to cadets at West Point in 1969: "He set an example for me in particular and the other POWs in the camp. He died for what he believed in."

5

James Butler
"Wild Bill" Hickok

No braver man ever drew a breath.

—*John Wesley Hardin, outlaw*

IF JAMES BUTLER HICKOK hadn't walked down the streets of Abilene, wearing a pair of ivory-handled Navy Colt revolvers, a novelist would have invented him. But Wild Bill Hickok was as real as they came in the Old West, a man of titanium stamp quick to defend himself with his fists or his pistols. Yet like so many of the men in these pages, he defended the meek and powerless.

Union cavalry scout. Wagon master. Plainsman. Lawman. Indian fighter. Hickok, a blue-gray-eyed, broad-shouldered man who stood more than six feet tall, was all of them, and when the truth about him is gleaned from the legendary chaff of fictive derring-do, we are left with a man of surpassing heroism. Hickok's life is so full of high-blown adventure and danger it sounds more like fiction than fact. Even biographic descriptions of his appearance border on the kind of prose one might read in a novel about some mythic icon of the past or a screenwriter's sketch of a western film hero.

"Physically he was a delight to look upon," wrote Elizabeth Custer, wife of the famous and ill-fated cavalry officer. Hickok was "tall, lithe, and free in every motion, he rode and walked as if every muscle was perfection, and the careless swing of his body as he moved seemed perfectly in keeping with the man, the country, the time in which he lived. I do not recall anything finer in the way of physical perfection than Wild Bill when he swung himself lightly from his saddle, and with graceful, swaying step, squarely set shoulders and well poised head approached our tent for orders."

Such was the awe with which Hickok was held by a woman who lived in an age when American men were awesome. Yet Hickok wasn't merely what women today would distastefully call eye candy. His physical prowess, audacity, and raw nerve, as well as his skill with a gun, were as sublime as his affecting appearance.

THE BIRTH OF A PLAINSMAN

JAMES BUTLER HICKOK was born in Troy Grove, Illinois, on May 26, 1837, to William Alonzo and Polly Butler Hickok. William was a Quaker who assisted escaping slaves, but he died when Wild Bill was just reaching what for the nineteenth-century frontier was manhood. He wasn't fifteen years old, but early on, James established a reputation for trouncing bullies.

According to biographer John Richard, writing for the Kansas Heritage Center Web site, "One day, while swimming with some friends in a stream that ran through the property, a local bully started picking on one of his friends. The bully frightened his friend and James, always a defender of the weak, promptly picked the bully up and then threw him into the water. The future character of the one eventually to be known as 'The Prince of the Pistoleers' was slowly emerging." Indeed

BUFFALO BILL HISTORICAL CENTER, CODY, WYOMING, P.71.1632

Known as "Prince of the Pistoleers," James Butler Hickok led one of the most thrilling lives in the annals of the American West. He also made one of the most enduring legends.

it was. Working at the Illinois and Michigan Canal, he tossed his employer in the river for mistreating a team of horses. "The pattern of his life was hardening into the lifelong habit of interposing himself between the oppressed and the oppressor," Richard observed. In 1867, he thrashed a man who insulted the wife of a friend and "added insult to his injury" by "jumping on his face with both feet."

As with many frontiersman of the time, Hickok was supposed to have killed a bear with a knife, but the provenance and veracity of the story are questionable. But it is not incompatible with the character of the man, and in any event Hickok served as wagonmaster, scout, and spy for the Union army and was involved in the border troubles between Kansas and Missouri during the War Between the States. As well, he guided the forces of Gen. Phillip H. Sheridan and was a close acquaintance of Gen. George Armstrong Custer, who spoke highly of the longhaired man who wore a grandiloquent mustache and buckskins and yet mostly traveled by mule.

Three stories from this phase of Hickok's career are illustrative of his nerve. During the War Between the States, at the battle of Pea Ridge in Arkansas, the sharpshooter supposedly killed thirty-five Confederates, and Union Gen. Samuel R. Curtis employed him as a spy. The accounts of his service vary, but he either enlisted in a ranger company under the command of Confederate Gen. Sterling Price and became an orderly on his staff, or he was captured as a spy, and such was his backbone that the general hired him on. Either way, Hickok infiltrated enemy lines at great peril. Spies, after all, are shot.

According to the first account, which has Hickok joining the Confederate side, Price ordered Hickok to deliver a dispatch to Gen. Joseph Shelby. Hickok, of course, planned to deliver the information to the Federals. His ruse? He challenged another man to a game of chicken to see who would ride closest to the Union lines. As the two approached the Federal lines, biographer Frank Wilstach reported, Hickok shouted to the men to hold their fire until he reached their lines. Realizing mischief was afoot, the Confederate challenger drew his pistol, but "Bill instantly sent a ball crashing into his brain."

The story might be apocryphal, but the truth remains that Hickok served on Price's staff and, at a minimum, escaped and returned to his command with information about the Rebel plans. One Yankee commander called Hickok and another scout "thrusting, daring and fearless men." Hickok, biographer Joseph G. Rosa reported, didn't kill the Indian warrior Black Kettle, as was widely reported, but another story of Hickok's fabled audacity and horsemanship demonstrates his fearlessness.

On April 19, 1867, Custer ordered the rough-and-ready plainsman to deliver a dispatch, requesting supplies, to a fort sixty miles away. Riding a mule and armed with a carbine, confident he was good for killing a dozen Indians on the way, Hickok not only delivered the dispatch but also returned with the answer that the wagons were on the way. He made the round-trip alone within hostile Indian territory. In 1868, when 350 Kiowa braves surrounded Hickok and a company of 40 men, the scout jumped atop his steed and galloped for help, shooting his way out of the trap.

GUNFIGHTER AND MARSHALL

YET IT wasn't his war exploits alone that burnished Hickok's reputation with the American public, which was eager for stories about the wild and wooly West and the cast-iron men driving cattle, policing towns, and killing Indians. He was known as the prince of the "pistoleers" for his prowess with a revolver, a reputation he deserved. Joseph G. Rosa records seven authenticated gunfights in which Hickok killed no more than ten men. Reports that he killed more than a hundred are highly dubious. Ten was plenty, and he killed them all in self-defense. Hickok was an expert marksman with his Navy Colts, a point in dispute that doesn't much matter because most of his gunfights occurred at close range. Contrary to one report, Hickok did not always aim for the head but rather the navel. "You may not make a fatal shot," the pistolero averred, "but he will get a shock that will paralize his brain and arm so much that the fight is all over." Hickok's prowess lay in his speed, but surviving seven gunfights with nary a scratch confirmed his ability to put a bullet on the target. "His skill in the use of the rifle and pistol was unerring," George A. Custer wrote.

Not that Hickok was averse to fisticuffs. Hickok's contemporary John Malone said that he was "the only frontiersman who would take his pistols off and fight a square fight with anyone who wanted to settle a dispute that way." Of course, if you didn't want to settle a dispute that way, Hickok could quickly draw his ivory-handled pistols.

One of Hickok's most famous gunfights occurred against the so-called McCanles gang, but the details are so murky no

Hickok was in numerous gunfights and likely conducted the first showdown in a public street. "His skill in the use of the rifle and pistol was unerring," George Armstrong Custer wrote.

BUFFALO BILL HISTORICAL CENTER, CODY, WYOMING, P.71.1650

one is sure whether Hickok killed anyone that day at Black Rock, Kansas, in 1861. But on July 21, 1865, Hickok participated in the first "high-noon" showdown of Hollywood myth, which many now mistakenly believe was the usual way gunfighters practiced their lethal profession. Hickok's nemesis was Dave Tutt, a former Confederate who landed in Springfield, Missouri, in 1864. The two men were acquainted; both were gamblers. A fight over a gambling debt and Hickok's pocket watch provoked their dispute.

The two were playing cards, with Hickok, according to one account, winning the princely sum of two hundred dollars. Tutt angrily demanded that Hickok pay him forty dollars owed for a horse trade, a request to which Hickok acceded. But then Tutt demanded thirty-five dollars for a previous gambling debt. No, Hickok said, the sum was twenty-five dollars, but he would check his "memorandum," and if Tutt were right, Hickok would cough up the thirty-five dollars. As collateral, Hickok put his pocket watch on the card table, and Tutt seized the timepiece until Hickok paid up.

The dispute continued into the next afternoon, and Tutt, according to Richard's account, bragged around town about taking Hickok's watch. He also said he would wear it in the town square. Hickok warned the man not to shame him, but at 6:00 p.m., Tutt walked into the square from the courthouse. Hickok approached from either the west or south, depending on which account one consults, and then warned Tutt not to go any farther. The men were about seventy-five yards apart. Tutt reached for his pistol, Hickok drew his, and history was made. Hickok's bullet hit Tutt squarely in the chest, and barely had the Reb fallen dead when Hickok wheeled to face Tutt's friends behind him.

"'Aren't you satisfied? Gentlemen,' cried Bill, as cool as an alligator," according to the famous account in *Harper's* magazine. "'Put up yer shootin'-irons or they'll be more dead men here.'"

So went the demise of Dave Tutt, and one wonders, by today's standards, why anyone would kill a man over a watch. It wasn't the watch. As Wilstach reports, Hickok's honor was at stake. "The whole matter seems piffling in the extreme, yet it is necessary to take into account that the frontier code was not like ours, and for Tutt to carry Bill's watch was a slur on the ability of the latter that would destroy his prestige in the community."

Another Hickok story, for instance, has the plainsman killing James "Dog" Kennedy in a gunfight at fifty feet. Kennedy shot first and missed Hickok. With his pistols cocked in their holsters, Hickok drew both and put a bullet in Kennedy's knee and another in his chest. Kennedy had accused Hickok of cheating at cards.

Today, a man is virtually required to surrender his honor on demand, to bear any slur not only to himself but also to his mother, wife, sisters, or family, even when their lives are at stake. The men of Hickok's time were not so enlightened, and thus it was that Hickok never shrank from standing up to a challenge. He didn't seek trouble, but when it found him, he put a quick end to it with brawn or bullets.

So it went for three ruffians who thought they could push him around, only this time it was Marshal Hickok of Hays City, Kansas, and the year was 1869. The first was Samuel Strawhan, a notorious desperado. Various accounts put him in Hays City for different reasons; Wilstach says he was there to "perforate" the plainsman. Whatever the case, Hickok was in a saloon on October 19 when Strawhan walked in. Just a few feet away from Hickok, Strawhan pulled his pistol, but Hickok saw him in the mirror. A Hickok bullet went through Strawhan's brain, and another bad man of the West went to Boot Hill. Rosa added that Strawhan and some men were wrecking a saloon, tossing the glasses outside to stop anyone from buying anything. Hickok showed up, and Strawhan threatened him with a piece of broken glass. So Hickok shot him dead.

A month later, two drunks from the U.S. Seventh Cavalry attacked Hickok at a saloon. The pair jumped him while he was talking to the bartender. One held Hickok's arms and pulled him to the floor while the other shoved a .44-caliber Remington to Hickok's ear. Unhappily for the assailants, the weapon misfired. Before he could recock, Hickok pulled his pistol, disabled the man who held him by striking him on the knee, then shot the gunman twice.

In December, Hickok faced Bill Mulvey, another outlaw. When Hickok tried to arrest the miscreant, Mulvey pulled two pistols and aimed at Hickok. "I can't beat that pair," Hickok said, according to Wilstach, quoting a famous account of the fight. "He backed off two or three steps and raised his hand protestingly."

"'Don't shoot him—he's only in fun!'" Hickok said to no one in particular.

Mulvey turned, expecting to find another deputy.

Hickok put a bullet in Mulvey's head. Rosa says the fight

took place in August and that Hickok drilled Mulvey "through the neck and lungs," but whichever story is true, Hickok's steel nerves never failed him. When danger was afoot in Hays City, Hickok was up and running to stop it.

Such was also true in Abilene, Kansas, where Hickok was marshal in 1871. A gambler named Phillip Coe operated a crooked faro game at the Bull's Head Saloon, which carried an explicit painting of a bull on its sign as well as paintings of naked ladies that offended Hickok's moral sensibilities. Wilstach claimed the crooked gambler Coe was dispatched to kill the legendary lawman. Whether one or both are true is of little matter. Coe and a few fellow Texans were wandering about town, unable to attend the nearby Dickenson County Fair because of the weather. It was October 5, about 9:00 p.m., Rosa reported, and the Texans were demanding that the bar patrons buy them drinks. This comports with Wilstach's account of the Texans carrying Jacob Karatosky, a merchant, into a saloon and being "permitted to set up the drinks."

Hickok and deputy Jim Williams, awaiting trouble at the Novelty, another watering hole, warned the Texans against carrying guns, but unsurprisingly, they ignored the advice. Hickok heard a shot outside the Alamo saloon, and when he investigated, the Texans and Coe were gathered outside. Standing just eight feet away, Coe, who claimed he shot a stray dog, challenged Hickok, firing twice. One shot either went through his clothes or zinged his side; the other hit the ground. Hickok shot Coe dead. Hearing the shots and disregarding Hickok's order to stay at the Novelty, deputy Williams came running with his pistol drawn. Hickok wheeled and fired. But he killed his friend. Angered at his tragic and irredeemable mistake, Hickok drove the drunken Texans out of town. It was Hickok's last gunfight.

A Showman Gets a Showman's End

FOR A time, Hickok joined Buffalo Bill's Wild West Show, and while in New York, he showed his mettle again, wrote Richard. "The long-haired frontiersman" wandered into a pool room, and some local toughs "thought they would have some sport with him." Putting it mildly, Richard reported, "one thing led to another," and the half-dozen rowdies "lay unconscious on the pool-room floor." One can only imagine what thing led to the inevitable result that Hickok was the only man left standing. "I got lost among the hostiles," he said after the incident.

But it wasn't long before Hickok was back in the country he loved, the West, where he met his demise in 1876, at age thirty-nine.

Hickok was at Nuttall & Man's No. 10 Saloon in Deadwood, South Dakota, pursuing his favorite avocation, poker, and did not get his customary seat with his back to the wall. Considering the kind of trouble his reputation invited, Hickok never sat with his back to a door or window for good reason. But this one night, one of the poker buddies took his seat, forcing the pistoleer to sit with his back to the door. On August 1, Rosa reported, he cleaned out a fellow named Jack McCall but gave him money for breakfast with a warning not to play if he didn't have the funds. Next day, McCall walked into the No. 10, stood behind Hickok, and put a bullet into his brain. The hero of the Plains died instantly. Various accounts say McCall sought revenge for Hickok's killing a brother or that McCall was drinking at the bar when he turned and killed Hickok. Others say he was a hired assassin. One account claimed that McCall was Samuel Strawhan's cousin, Strawhan being one of the outlaws Hickok killed.

In a bit of romantic lore, the story goes that Hickok held black aces and eights with a queen or jack of diamonds kicker

In 1873, Hickok (second from the left) posed with (left to right) Eugene Overton, Buffalo Bill Cody, Texas Jack Omohundro, and Elisha Green while the five were appearing in Ned Buntline's play *Scouts of the Prairie*. Three years later, Hickok was gunned down from behind in Deadwood, South Dakota.

when he met his ignominious fate. This is unauthenticated, but the story of the Dead Man's Hand is widely repeated. It shows up as the hand Liberty Valance (Lee Marvin) held before his gunfight with Ransom Stoddard (Jimmy Stewart) in *The Man Who Shot Liberty Valance*. If the story isn't true, it should be.

Contrary to some opinion, Hickok never started a fight, although he finished many and permanently so for some of the men unwise enough to push their luck. As one admirer said, "It can never be said of Bill that he was the unprovoked assailant of any man."

Hickok "had his faults," including gambling and drunkenness, said fellow scout Jack Crawford, who, like Hickok, struck out to hunt for gold in Deadwood. "Yet even when full of the vile libel of the name of whiskey which was dealt over the bars at exorbitant prices, he was gentle as a child, unless aroused to anger by intended insults. . . . He was loyal in his friendship, generous to a fault, and invariably espoused the cause of the weaker against the stronger one in a quarrel."

"Having acquired a reputation as a 'shot' and as a fearless man in early life," Rosa quoted another contemporary, "he was time and again called upon to defend himself by killing men against whom he had no ill will whatever." Said Hickok himself, "That I have killed men I admit, but never unless in absolute self defense or in the performance of an official duty. I never, in all my life, took any mean advantage of an enemy. Yet understand, I never allowed a man to get the drop on me."

Hickok defended the weak against the powerful, including abused animals. Once he stopped a lynching. He loved children, and they loved him, and not surprisingly, so did women. Elizabeth Custer, one of his many admirers, said that Easterners most likely misunderstood the genuine character of some of the men who explored, settled, and civilized the West. They weren't merely gamblers and outlaws with a taste for strong drink, and lots of it at that. Rather, they were good men and gentlemen. "I remember watching Wild Bill," she wrote,

> as he reported at the Commanding Officers' tent to get despatches from my husband, and wishing with all my heart that I could go with him. I know this must seem strange to people in the States, whose ideas of scouts are made up from stories of shooting affrays, gambling, lynching and outlawry. I should have felt myself safe to go any distance with these men whom my husband employed as bearers of despatches. I have never known women treated with such reverence.

During an interview in 1936, Richard writes, an old woman from Kansas recalled Hickok, then a marshal in Abilene, visiting her farm and bringing candy to her and her siblings. Once, when her family had not been warned, as was usual, to head for town because of an approaching cattle drive, Hickok rode to her farm to stand watch over the passing cowboys. "Oh, I tell you, I tell you," she recalled, "he was a grand man was Marshal Hickok, a grand man!"

Hickok also was a dangerous man, but only to those looking for trouble. If they found Hickok, they got it. A man of dauntless daring, Hickok was thrust into circumstances requiring lethal violence. It was the American frontier, during the bloody border war between Kansas Jayhawkers and Missouri Ruffians, the War Between the States, the savage campaign against the Plains Indians, and the rough cowtowns where rowdy, violent men were put in their place not with psychotherapy and anger management but with a .44-caliber Colt Navy.

Perhaps what makes Hickok an example from which to learn is his undiluted courage, particularly in defending the weak and defenseless. That his life ended, not in a fair fight, but with a shot from behind from a coward is testimony to his fighting prowess. Face to face, few if any could best him. And that is what makes him the quintessential American man.

6

Lou Gehrig

I would not have traded two minutes of the joy and the grief with that man for two decades of anything with another.

—*Eleanor Gehrig*

No man is a hero to his wife.

The aphorism is rooted in the seventeenth-century proverb, "No man is a hero to his valet," from Mademoiselle A. M. Bigot de Cornuel, an observation that, on meeting our heroes, we find they have feet of clay. Like us, they put their pants on one leg at a time.

But maybe that wasn't the case with Lou Gehrig, the man they called "Gibraltar in Cleats," mythic giant of the New York Yankees in the era of Ruth and Pipp and McCarthy and Lazzeri. If any twentieth-century athlete qualifies as a man among men, it's Gehrig, the polar opposite of the modern athlete, represented in either the criminal, the crybaby, or the steroidally fortified multimillionaire. "He was beautiful," Eleanor Gehrig wrote. "Six feet tall, 205 pounds, sturdy as a rock and innocent as a waif."

The innocent waif was born June 19, 1903, Heinrich Ludwig Gehrig into a rapidly changing world. Skyscrapers rose to the heavens in New York City. Henry Ford began the Ford Motor Company. Marie Curie won the Nobel Prize. Edwin S. Porter produced *The Great Train Robbery*. Thomas Hunt Morgan discovered chromosomes on genes, and the Wright Brothers flew. Other famous Americans born that year? Clare Boothe Luce, Bing Crosby, and Bob Hope. In England, George Orwell.

Gehrig's two sisters and a brother died before they reached the age of two. Lou's mother believed baseball was a "waste of time" that would "never get you anywhere," a "game for bummers." If you believe the film *Pride of the Yankees*, she wanted him to follow in the steps of his Uncle Otto, an engineer. Lou attended Columbia University on a football scholarship to study engineering, but he made his mark on the baseball diamond. It wasn't long before the Yankees came knocking, and in 1925, after a few years in the minors, Gehrig donned number 4. "Larrupin' Lou" batted fourth to Babe Ruth's third.

His statistics are legendary. He posted a lifetime .340 batting average and blasted 493 home runs. His batting average in the World Series was .361, with his best against Chicago in 1932, .529. Most impressive of all, he played 2,130 consecutive games, a record that stood until Cal Ripken of the Baltimore Orioles broke it on September 6, 1995. Gehrig played through broken fingers, sprained ankles, bruises, contusions, and just about every other imaginable ache and pain. X-rays showed seventeen broken or fractured bones in his hands, particularly the glove hand, many of which healed without the intervention of a doctor. He was one tough German.

All these facts about Gehrig add to his luster; they burnish his image as the kind of hero men can only dream of emulating. But it wasn't Gehrig's extraordinary athleticism that accounts for his inclusion here, nor is it why Gehrig is held in mythic regard. Rather, it was Gehrig's determined face while handling the adversity of a terminal disease.

Gehrig played ball for nearly fourteen years without a break, but in the season of 1938, his muscles began to fail. In *Pride of the Yankees,* it begins with a crick in his shoulder. Of course, he just shook it off. Just another day at the ballpark. But it was more than that.

The Iron Horse deteriorated rapidly. His teammates didn't know why, but they saw what was happening to this incredible specimen of manhood. His batting average plummeted 56 points to .295. A mystified Joe DiMaggio watched Gehrig miss nineteen straight cuts in batting practice. One afternoon he fell while trying to put on his pants in the clubhouse. Another time, he fell off a bench in the clubhouse when he got up to look out the window. Attending a pro-golf tournament in Florida, friends noticed he didn't wear cleats to walk in the grass as he usually would, but tennis shoes. He had good reason. He couldn't pick up his feet, which slowed his base running. Nor could he move his hands fast enough to catch balls fired across the diamond to him at first base. In the ultimate affront to a hitter of Gehrig's clout, a batter whose average hadn't dropped below .300 since 1925, Lefty Grove of the Boston Red Sox walked Joe DiMaggio so he could face the ailing first baseman. Gehrig was an easy out.

At home, Eleanor watched the decay, wondering what was happening to her Luke. Just a slump at the plate, they said. He just needs a little rest, everyone agreed. He dropped kitchen china inexplicably. He fell frequently when he and Eleanor went ice-skating, a favorite pastime. This, she asked herself, is a slump? Finally, on May 2, 1939, he took himself out of the lineup. A few weeks later, Eleanor scheduled an appointment at the Mayo Clinic. Dr. Harold Habein knew what was wrong as soon as Gehrig inched into his office. "When [he] entered my office," the doctor said, "and I saw the shuffling gait, and his overall expression, then shook his hand, I knew." The Iron

NATIONAL BASEBALL HALL OF FAME LIBRARY, COOPERSTOWN, NY

Lou Gehrig played in 2,130 consecutive games (a major league record that lasted until 1995) and posted a lifetime .340 batting average and blasted 493 home runs. He played through a variety a injuries, including seventeen broken or fractured bones, many of them in his glove hand.

Man had amyotrophic lateral sclerosis, after that, forever known as Lou Gehrig's disease. He was thirty-six.

The disease is a death sentence, although Lou didn't know right away. He died on June 2, 1941, sixteen years to the day he replaced Wally Pipp at first base.

A Modern Ballplayer

But before describing how Gehrig handled his tragic destiny, listen to another story about a modern ballplayer and how he handled what anyone would consider a disappointment, although certainly no colossal tragedy worthy of the rebarbative display to which the public was subjected.

The player's name is unimportant; it serves no purpose to ridicule the man. Let's just say he was, in his own mind, a player of Gehrig's caliber. He expected induction into the Baseball Hall of Fame.

Such was his conceit that he invited reporters to his home the day he knew the telephone call would come. They gathered in his kitchen, expecting, as did he, word of his elevation to baseball's Valhalla. But the news from Cooperstown wasn't what he expected, and he was not among the chosen few. Understandably, he was disappointed, as any good ball player would be. But he wasn't just disappointed. He was angry, feeling unjustly deprived of something he so richly deserved. What followed was a display of puerile histrionics: a foot-stomping, childish tantrum.

The *New York Times* reported: "[He] described how his wife . . . planned a surprise party for him and instead wept when they discovered he had not been elected. That caused [him] to cry, too. There were reporters [there] poised to witness a celebratory scene as he was finally honored as one of baseball's elite players. But it did not occur and tears flowed."

"He admitted to being devastated," the *Times* continued, "because he felt the expectation of being elected more than ever this year. He spoke about how it would torment him if his [aging father] did not live to see him enshrined." In complaining about the snub from baseball's pantheon of heroes, the player said, "I'd like to ask any of the sportswriters did any of them ever get behind the plate and catch for nine innings?"

Sitting behind a plate for nine innings? How about a death sentence before age forty? "Devastated?" You're "devastated" when your nine-year-old boy gets cancer. You're "devastated" when a drunk driver kills your daughter. But not when the Hall of Fame says it isn't your turn. What would Gehrig have said? Probably something like this: "Well, boys, you can't win 'em all. Let's toast the guys who made it. They were better men than me."

Since inducted at Cooperstown, the player is an example of modern American manhood, particularly the modern athlete, and we can thank the news media for depicting the specimen in all its glory. He is a perfect example of what we don't want our sons to be: conceited, arrogant, and spiteful, believing himself more deserving than someone else. Jesus Christ said the first will be last, and the last will be first. This fellow did not agree. One can only imagine how he would have handled the news Gehrig received in the flower of his manhood.

A Good Guy, a Great Man

Now, consider a few things about Gehrig, and you'll know he handled what most would say is a cosmic injustice and, in an unguarded moment, perhaps a divine injustice.

As with modern athletes, in the old days, an athlete's talents and popularity were measured in commercial endorsements. Lou endorsed a breakfast cereal called Huskies, and appearing on Robert Ripley's *Believe or Not* radio program, he was supposed to plug the product. "Well, Lou, what helps you hit all those home runs?" Ripley asked.

"A heaping bowlful of Wheaties!" Lou replied. Huh? Wheaties? Lou returned the thousand dollars he was paid to pitch Huskies, then he returned to the show and plugged the cereal correctly.

"Lou," biographer Richard Bak wrote, "believed in doing the right thing." He invested all of his life savings for his parents after he married Eleanor and handed them the deed to a new house and new car.

And we know he was tough. He played through those seventeen broken bones for more than a decade, including a thumb and toe, as well as back spasms, that would have dropped a less resilient man. He once played a game the day after a pitcher beaned him unconscious. Next day, he wore an oversized cap to accommodate the grapefruit on his noggin. He smashed three triples.

It wasn't easy for Gehrig to pull himself out of the lineup, but when he did, no one had to ask. He told manager Joe McCarthy: "For the good of the team, Joe. Nobody has to tell me how bad I've been and how much of a drawback I've been to the club. . . . [T]he time has come for me to quit."

By all accounts, Gehrig was resolute and valiant. When his batting average dropped, he took a three-thousand-dollar pay cut without complaint. He simply worked all the harder to

Gehrig was known as "Gibraltar in Cleats" and the "Iron Man." On May 2, 1939, at age thirty-five, he surprised the baseball world when he took himself out of the Yankees lineup. Said his friend, shortstop Sam Jones, "Lou was the kind of boy that if you had a son, he's the kind of person you'd like your son to be."

recover his prowess at the plate. He struggled mightily against the unknown. One account has Gehrig eating grass to conquer the creeping paralysis. Eleanor dutifully pulled it from the ground to make some sort of soup. He thought the vitamins would cure his disease. They didn't.

GEHRIG FACES DEATH

ON JULY 4, 1939, Gehrig delivered the most famous oration ever by an American athlete. Such was its emotive puissance it is known as baseball's Gettysburg Address. It was Lou Gehrig Day at Yankee Stadium, and all his teammates, current and former, were there to honor him. That included the Babe, with

July 4, 1939, was Lou Gehrig Day at Yankee Stadium. Crippled with amyotrophic lateral sclerosis, Gehrig told the crowd that he considered himself the "luckiest man on the face of the earth." The disease killed him on June 2, 1941, sixteen years to the day after he replaced Wally Pipp at first base.

NATIONAL BASEBALL HALL OF FAME LIBRARY, COOPERSTOWN, NY

whom he hadn't spoken in years because Gehrig's mother (or wife, in some accounts) made an unflattering remark about the accouterments of Ruth's daughter. Sid Mercer, a veteran sportswriter who served as master of ceremonies, told the sixty thousand adoring fans that Gehrig was too moved to speak. The crowd wanted none of it. "We want Gehrig!" they roared. "We want Gehrig!" And Gehrig went to the microphone:

> Fans, for the past two weeks you have been reading about a bad break I got. Yet today, I consider myself the luckiest man on the face of the earth. I have been in ballparks for seventeen years and I have never received anything but kindness and encouragement from you fans.

Gehrig continued talking, but not about himself and his stellar career. Rather, he spoke about his teammates and pals and what they meant to him. And then he spoke about the men he played against, and how grateful he was that they sent him a gift. "That's something," he said. "Sure, I'm lucky."

That doesn't sound anything like the catcher who assembled sportswriters at his home to get the news about his induction into the Hall of Fame and then threw a tantrum when he heard the news that he wasn't ready for Cooperstown.

Gehrig's humility is one of the hallmarks of genuine masculinity. Ever humble, even in his final appearance on the baseball diamond where he was a champion, he didn't speak of himself or his awful fate. Rather, he told the assembled throng that he was lucky, then expressed his admiration for others, diverting the spotlight to them. He praised his mom and dad. He praised his loving wife. He even praised his adoring fans. He spoke about everyone but himself, and when he did speak of himself, it was only in the context of others: how lucky he was to have known them and for them to love him.

LOU GEHRIG'S FAREWELL SPEECH
YANKEE STADIUM
JULY 4, 1939

Fans, for the past two weeks you have been reading about a bad break I got. Yet today I consider myself the luckiest man on the face of the earth. I have been in ballparks for seventeen years and have never received anything but kindness and encouragement from you fans.

Look at these grand men. Which of you wouldn't consider it the highlight of his career to associate with them for even one day?

Sure, I'm lucky. Who wouldn't consider it an honor to have known Jacob Ruppert—also the builder of baseball's greatest empire, Ed Barrow—to have spent the next nine years with that wonderful little fellow Miller Huggins—then to have spent the next nine years with that outstanding leader, that smart student of psychology—the best manager in baseball today, Joe McCarthy!

Sure, I'm lucky. When the New York Giants, a team you would give your right arm to beat, and vice versa, sends you a gift, that's something! When everybody down to the groundskeepers and those boys in white coats remember you with trophies, that's something.

When you have a wonderful mother-in-law who takes sides with you in squabbles against her own daughter, that's something. When you have a father and mother who work all their lives so that you can have an education and build your body, it's a blessing! When you have a wife who has been a tower of strength and shown more courage than you dreamed existed, that's the finest I know.

So I close in saying that I might have had a tough break—but I have an awful lot to live for!

Was he afraid? Undoubtedly. Eddie Rickenbacker said that courage is conquering fear, not the absence of it. Gehrig picked up the hand he was dealt and played it like a man.

Aside from showing us how a real man faces death, Gehrig was no criminal, as are so many of today's athletes. He was never convicted of a crime, nor ever accused of one. He never spit on an umpire or throttled his coach. He was no multimillion-dollar crybaby. Today, such "men" seem to be the rule, not the exception. Gehrig, a sportswriter once wrote, was "unspoiled, without the remotest vestige of ego, vanity or conceit."

Likening him to the public image of the man who played him in *Pride of the Yankees*, Gary Cooper, another writer called him "a figure of unimpeachable integrity, massive and incorruptible, a hero. Today, both are seen as paradigms of manly virtue. Decent and God-fearing, yet strongly charismatic and powerful." The difference between the two, however, was that Gehrig genuinely embodied those traits.

Gehrig would be out of place in modern sports. It seems as if newspapers carry a daily report of millionaire athletes— particularly the rotten, criminal timber of the NBA and the NFL—landing in jail. Few if any modern athletes are "innocent" or "massive and incorruptible" or "unimpeachable" or "unspoiled, without the remotest vestige of ego, vanity or conceit." Gehrig was.

One of Gehrig's teammates, shortstop Sam Jones, paid the Iron Man the highest compliment any man could hope to receive: "Lou was the kind of boy that if you had a son, he's the kind of person you'd like your son to be."

Any son's father knows what kind of tribute that is, the kind of tribute few modern athletes deserve. It says, in so many words, there goes a real man.

7

Audie Murphy

[Audie Murphy was] the finest soldier I have ever seen
in my entire military career.

—*Gen. Keith Ware*

Y OU KNOW WHO Audie Murphy is, don't you?"

The question came as I was telling a co-worker and friend,
a man passionate about history, some remarkable things I
learned about Murphy while writing this book. Sitting nearby
was a recent college graduate, the target of my question.

"Never heard of him," he answered unsurprisingly.

"Young people today hardly know who Audie Murphy
was," Don Graham wrote in *No Name on the Bullet,* his wonderful biography. "Pressed, they may think he's Eddie Murphy's
brother." But that is unsurprising, for we no longer honor the
kind of man Audie Murphy was. "We prefer video fantasy,"
Graham wrote, "Rambo—a kind of MTV celebration of American machismo." But Murphy, Graham correctly noted, "could
have had Sylvester Stallone for breakfast. Audie Murphy was
the real thing, not some pumped-up, aerobicized, celluloid pa-
looka."

Although Murphy was a movie star, he was indeed the real

thing. So were many of his fellow stars. Back then, Hollywood hadn't been feminized. It may have been the world of make-believe, but many of the actors were real men and projected the image on film. James Arness, Charles Bronson, Eddie Albert, and Lee Marvin all fought in World War II. Other actors, including Clark Gable and Jimmy Stewart, twice decorated with the Distinguished Flying Cross, left lucrative acting careers to serve their country.

But Murphy was the most celebrated war hero of all. Decorated thirty-three times during World War II, he received the Medal of Honor for action at the Colmar Pocket in France in January 1945. And even after the war, Murphy's courage carried him through more than one scrape.

EARLY LIFE

LIKE ANDREW JACKSON, Murphy was raised in hardscrabble country, but for the latter it was Greenville, Texas, about fifty miles northeast of Dallas. Born June 20, 1925, and descended from Scots-Irish Southerners, including Confederate and World War I veterans, he was one of nine children. Murphy's father, a sharecropper, wasn't much concerned with provender for his large brood.

The Murphys were dirt poor. Indeed, they couldn't afford the dirt. They survived in grinding poverty, unlike the "poverty" we hear about today, which somehow permits welfare recipients to buy televisions, video games, and lottery tickets. At one miserable point, the Murphys lived in a train car, which provides a sadly authentic picture of Audie Murphy's penurious childhood. "I never had just 'fun,'" he wrote. "I am one Texan boy who never had a pair of cowboy boots. I am one native-born and native-bred American male who actually doesn't know the rules of our national pastime—baseball.

I never had time to play or the paraphernalia you play it with. I never had a bike. It was a full-time job just existing."

A good student, Murphy finished the fifth grade and, in 1939, left home. His father vanished in 1940, and shortly after that, his mother died. In childhood, he developed the keen senses and wits that served well in battle during World War II. A crack shot, Murphy killed rabbits with a slingshot. Once, a friend loaned him a .22-caliber rifle and eight bullets. Murphy returned from a hunt with four rabbits and handed four bullets back to the friend. He could shoot a camouflaged squirrel out of bushy tree and could put a slug in a bounding rabbit from a car. He was also a scrapper, unafraid of fisticuffs with a bigger kid. One teacher called him her "Fighting Irishman."

On December 7, 1941, when the Japanese bombed Pearl Harbor, Murphy was sixteen and itching to enlist. "They can't do that," he told the postman, asking where Pearl Harbor was. On his eighteenth birthday, just five feet five inches tall and 112 pounds, he rushed to the Marine Corps recruiting station, but "the corps was looking for men, italicized," he wrote in his autobiography, *To Hell and Back*. "A sergeant glanced over my skinny physique. My weight did not measure up to Leatherneck standards." Likewise with the paratroops. Too small, the recruiting sergeant said, "Load up on bananas and milk before weighing in." And likely, they thought him too young; he probably looked fourteen, not eighteen. Finally, the army infantry took him, and he made a mark unknown in the annals of modern warfare.

WORLD WAR II AND THE MEDAL OF HONOR

MURPHY'S EXPLOITS in World War II are the unalloyed metal that make a legend. Like many recipients of the Medal of Honor, Murphy fought with such fearlessness, daring, and prowess, the story is hard to believe. If he were a character in a novel, you would dismiss the book as incredulous.

Murphy was a killing machine. Any German who faced him *mano a mano* was doomed, and many more who fought against him in squads, platoons, or companies wound up dead as well. Murphy's battlefield heroics are, using another trite formulation, too numerous to mention here, but those that invited the nation's three highest combat decorations exemplify Murphy's bravery in nearly two years of front-line combat.

Murphy's war began in Italy in 1943, where his comrades quickly learned he was an exceptional soldier. He earned a Bronze Star in the landing at Anzio. His fame rose from action in France, and from the moment Murphy landed near St. Tropez with the storied Third Infantry Division, part of Operation Anvil, his combat exploits were beyond extraordinary.

On day one at Ramatuelle in September, he wiped out a German machine-gun nest at the top of a hill, killing two Germans. Another fired on his position. Murphy and a buddy, Lattie Tipton, whom Murphy claimed was the best shot and bravest man he knew, moved through a ditch. Two Germans surprised the men and shot off a piece of Tipton's ear. Unfazed, he whirled and killed them at point-blank range with two shots from his carbine. Continuing to move through the ditch, as Murphy tells the story in *To Hell and Back,* Murphy and Tipton came under attack from another machine-gun nest and grenades. They found the nest, "putting a blast of fire on the gun crew," then rushed the hole. They killed two Germans with head shots and leaped into the lair just as another German machine-gun opened fire. The men then tossed hand grenades at that position and emptied their carbines. Two Germans help up a white flag to surrender.

"They're waving a handkerchief," Tipton said. "I'll go get 'em."

"Keep down," Murphy warned. "You can't trust them."

"Murphy, you're getting to be a plumb cynic," he said. "They've had enough."

When Tipton stood up, the Germans drilled him; the perfidy sent Murphy into a blind rage. As Murphy laid his dead mate under a cork tree, a machine-gun nest got Murphy in its sights. In the nick of time, he jumped back into the hole and tossed a grenade, killing the Germans who were about to fire. Murphy dashed for their pit, grabbed its weapon, and stormed up the hill toward the Germans who killed Tipton, firing madly. He killed them both. Then he returned to his friend, sat down, and, he recalled, "bawl[ed] like a baby." For his actions that day, Murphy received the Distinguished Service Cross, the nation's second-highest decoration for bravery.

On October 2, 1944, Murphy saved the life of Lt. Col. Keith Ware, who received the Medal of Honor for heroism at Cleurie Quarry, France. Ware's small patrol was pinned down, but Murphy had secretly followed it, telling a friend years later, "I figured those gentlemen were going to run into trouble; so I tagged along about 25 yards to their rear, to watch the stampede." Ware's biography at the Arlington National Cemetery Web site reports, "As the German machine gunner was about to finish off Ware and the patrol, Murphy stepped into the open just eight yards from the enemy. Murphy's famous luck was with him as the enemy gun barrel caught some brush as it swung around. Murphy finished off all eight ambushers with two grenades and his carbine in less than 30 seconds." Four of the Germans were dead; three wounded.

Murphy received the Silver Star for the action then received a second three days later near Le Tholy after inflicting fifty German casualties, including fifteen killed. His citation reads: "First Lieutenant MURPHY, carrying an SCR 536 radio, crawled fifty yards under severe enemy machine gun and rifle fire, to a point 200 yards from strongly entrenched enemy who had prevented further advance. Despite machine gun and rifle bullets that hit as close as a foot to him, First Lieutenant MUR-PHY directed artillery fire upon enemy positions for an hour."

Murphy, who received battlefield promotions to second and then first lieutenant, was also a deadly hunter on the battlefield, seeking and killing German snipers. But the action for which he is most famous occurred on January 26 at Holtzwihr, France.

Badly outnumbered by an attacking German force of two hundred men and six tanks, Murphy and his men, with two tank destroyers, one of which was disabled, were dug in at the edge of some woods. The ground was covered with nearly a foot of snow; overnight Murphy's hair had frozen to the ground. As the Germans approached, they smashed the second tank destroyer, killing three of its crew. Murphy ordered his men back to the woods, but the Texan stayed behind, firing with his carbine and directing artillery fire over the field telephone. When he emptied the carbine, he noticed the burning tank destroyer with a "perfectly good machine gun." Taking the phone, Murphy dashed to the flaming hulk, pulled off a dead GI, and sprang into action with the .50-caliber.

"How close are they to your position?" inquired a voice over the radio.

"Just hold the phone and I'll let you talk to one of [them]."

The Germans were a football field away; a German 88, the most feared artillery piece in the Wehrmacht's arsenal, hit the tank destroyer, which was full of gasoline and ammo and primed to explode. Miraculously, it merely burned as the minutes ticked by with the angry fire of Murphy's machine gun. Smoke from the burning hulk, which carried the ghastly smell of smoldering flesh, shrouded his position. For more than an hour, the Germans attacked him from three sides. His deadly gunfire from behind the billowing curtain of smoke threw

Audie Murphy was the most-decorated American soldier of World War II. Yet he had been deemed too small to pass muster with navy and marine recruiters when he tried to enlist after the attack on Pearl Harbor. Eventually, the army took him. Above he receives the Medal of Honor from Maj. Gen. "Iron Mike" O'Daniel.

them into confusion. At one harrowing point, a gust of wind cleared the smoke momentarily, and Murphy spotted a dozen Germans in a ditch just thirty yards away. When he spun his gun around, the smoke wafted into his line of fire again, obscuring the enemy troops, who were nearly upon him. When it cleared, they were a mere ten yards away. He mowed them down. "Partridges huddled in a ditch," he recalled.

On the phone, Murphy, with a leg wounded, called in more artillery fire to land just fifty yards from his position.

"Are you all right?" the radioman on the other end asked.

"I'm all right, sergeant. What are your post-war plans?"

The American barrage killed more Germans and sent the tanks heading back to Holtzwihr.

But Murphy called in one last correction.

"That's your own position!" the radioman exclaimed.

"I don't give a damn!" Murphy bellowed back.

Murphy continued fighting until his ammunition was exhausted, then he returned to his men, refused medical treatment, and organized a counterattack. His actions, his Medal of Honor citation says, prevented the encirclement and destruction of his company. In that one action, he had killed or wounded 50 German soldiers. When the war was over, he had killed nearly 250 enemy soldiers.

Later asked why he took on the Germans alone, Murphy replied, "I saw no reason for any more men to be killed when one man could do the job."

After the war, Murphy became an actor. Ironically, having been a combat soldier of exceptional skill and unparalleled courage, one of his first starring roles was in *The Red Badge of Courage,* which required him to play a Union soldier who flees the battlefield under fire. Costar Bill Mauldin is to the left.

THE AUDIE MURPHY RESEARCH FOUNDATION

AUDIE IN HOLLYWOOD

AFTER THE war, Murphy befriended actor Jimmy Cagney, who brought the war hero to Hollywood, where he began a long career, mostly in Westerns. Murphy wrote the critically acclaimed *To Hell and Back*, which itself became a film in which Audie played himself.

Murphy was a humble man. He didn't care much for medals and once said, "I never liked being called the 'most decorated soldier.' There were so many guys who should have gotten medals and never did—guys who were killed." He added, "The real heroes were the ones with the wooden crosses." He doesn't mention his battle decorations in his book, and he omitted the heroic action that saved Ware's life. He was honest about his fear, which is "right there beside you" in combat. But he was quick to anger, and he never let another man threaten or insult him. In that regard, he was of Jacksonian kidney. The difference was that Murphy lived in the twentieth century, not the nineteenth.

Measured by modern standards, his postwar deeds, as biographer Graham records them, seem nearly psychopathic. But better to take them for what they are: the actions of a man who would not be insulted or put upon, who expected to be treated with simple decency. He was a defender of the weak, an implacable foe of criminals and bullies.

Just after he returned from the war, Graham writes, Murphy unwisely picked up a hitchhiker near Vickery, outside Dallas. The hitchhiker was about six feet two inches tall and 190 pounds. Murphy thought he was a veteran. On entering Murphy's car, he shoved what he claimed was a .45-caliber pistol into Murphy's ribs. The man made the mistake of smacking Murphy, who, in the ensuing struggle, discovered the hitchhiker's ruse with the gun. Murphy kicked him out of the car and jumped on him. "I was so doggone scared I didn't hardly know what I was doing," he said, "and we fought for about 10 minutes and finally he didn't get up anymore."

On another occasion, driving along Ventura Boulevard in Hollywood, he saw two ruffians swerve their car near some kids on motor scooters. Audie pulled up and warned the reckless motorists to stop before someone got hurt. At the next light, the bullies, each double the size of the short Celt, pulled up and challenged him. Once out of their cars, director John Huston explained the story, "These two guys came at him, and Audie would knock one down and then the other one, and one would get up while the other was being knocked down until he had them both down and kicked the living s—t out of them."

At a Beverly Hills party, a guest was making a nuisance of himself. Murphy approached him twice and asked him to be more considerate of the other guests. Both times he was re-buffed. So Audie approached him again and told him to leave. The man was belligerent, but after one look at Murphy's eyes, he left. Those steel gray eyes, Graham wrote, "were the thing that everybody remembered. They were cold, almost deadly."

Unsurprisingly, and despite being an actor, Murphy didn't think much of Hollywood tough guys. He was always adept with a gun, which helped in the Westerns. Around the movie set, he was fastest on the draw, so fast his hand was a blur when photographed. Actor Hugh O'Brien, television's Wyatt Earp in the 1950s, fancied himself the fastest gunslinger in show business. The last gunfighter killed by one of John Wayne's cinematic bullets in *The Shootist*, he challenged Murphy to draw.

Sure, Murphy said. "I'll tell you what. You get real bullets in your gun and I'll get real bullets in mine, and we'll have a go at it." Wisely, O'Brien declined.

Murphy was a heavy gambler after the war, a bad habit that kept him in debt. One day at the racetrack, he was read-

Murphy and Hugh O'Brien starred in 1953's *Drums Across the River.* O'Brien believed he was the fastest gun in Hollywood and challenged Murphy to a contest. Audie suggested they load their weapons with live ammunition. O'Brien wisely declined.

ing the racing form, but he glanced up as two women walked by. He quickly went back to the form, oblivious to anything but handicapping the ponies. "About five minutes later," the story goes in Graham's account:

Here comes a big Dago guy about two hundred and something pounds and he says, "Hey, next time my wife ever comes here again and you make eyes at her . . ."

"Are you through?" Murphy replied.

"No, I'll tear your head off."

So Audie just leaned back and pulled out this gun and laid it right here and said, "I killed three-hundred fifty of you guys; one more wouldn't make any difference."

THE AUDIE MURPHY RESEARCH FOUNDATION

Murphy rode tall in the saddle in many westerns. In 1956, he starred with Jimmy Stewart (right)—recipient of two Distinguished Flying Crosses during World War II—in *Night Passage*. Stewart played a respected law-abiding brother to Murphy's wayward character (hence the white and black hats).

On more than one occasion, Murphy's mercurial temper got him in trouble, the worst being a charge of attempted murder against a dog trainer, who at more than six feet tall and nearly two hundred pounds, towered over Murphy. Murphy had given his girlfriend a German shepherd, and when the dog trainer went to her home to work the dog, he whipped it with a tree branch. She protested and demanded he depart, she testified at trial. Then they fought and he grabbed her inappropriately. Murphy went to the trainer's home with a friend, a scuffle ensued, and he supposedly fired a gun at the man. A jury acquitted him, and reading the story, the incident sounds like another instance of Murphy cleaning up the floor with a bully.

Tom Brokaw, the NBC newsman who wrote the foreword

to a recent edition of *To Hell and Back,* remembers the incident differently and says that Murphy was never charged. But Brokaw's report is similar to Graham's on one count: Murphy didn't want anyone thinking he couldn't hit a target the size of the dog trainer. On emerging from the police station, a reporter asked, "Audie, did you shoot at that guy?" Replied Audie, "If I had, do you think I would have missed?"

REMEMBER MURPHY

A FAIR appraisal of Murphy's postwar deeds might suggest a psychologically troubled man. To some degree, he was. He suffered nightmares and became addicted to sleeping pills, but ever the tenacious warrior, he locked himself in a hotel room and defeated the addiction. He candidly discussed the psychological damage war inflicts on a man, openly trying to help other veterans overcome what was then called battle fatigue and now called post-traumatic stress disorder. War took its toll on Murphy and thousands of other combat veterans. But we focus here on his triumphs, not his tragedies; on his fortitude, not his foibles.

Murphy may be the greatest American war hero ever. He rose from seemingly hopeless poverty to become the most storied fighting man of the twentieth century. His exploits stand up with the greatest in our history: Jackson at Horseshoe Bend, Crockett at the Alamo, Lee at Cerro Gordo and Chapultepec, Forrest in the War Between the States, York in World War I, Burke in Korea, and Versace in Vietnam. Yet our children, our sons in particular, don't know him. Indeed, Graham wrote, some Americans forgot him before he died.

On May 28, 1971, when his plane crashed into Brush Mountain near Roanoke, Virginia, killing all aboard, a reporter called a Veterans of Foreign Wars post for a comment about

AUDIE MURPHY'S CITATION FOR
THE MEDAL OF HONOR

2d Lt. Murphy commanded Company B, which was attacked by 6 tanks and waves of infantry. 2d Lt. Murphy ordered his men to withdraw to prepared positions in a woods, while he remained forward at his command post and continued to give fire directions to the artillery by telephone. Behind him, to his right, 1 of our tank destroyers received a direct hit and began to burn. Its crew withdrew to the woods. 2d Lt. Murphy continued to direct artillery fire which killed large numbers of the advancing enemy infantry. With the enemy tanks abreast of his position, 2d Lt. Murphy climbed on the burning tank destroyer, which was in danger of blowing up at any moment, and employed its .50 caliber machine gun against the enemy. He was alone and exposed to German fire from 3 sides, but his deadly fire killed dozens of Germans and caused their infantry attack to waver. The enemy tanks, losing infantry support, began to fall back. For an hour the Germans tried every available weapon to eliminate 2d Lt. Murphy, but he continued to hold his position and wiped out a squad which was trying to creep up unnoticed on his right flank. Germans reached as close as 10 yards, only to be mowed down by his fire. He received a leg wound, but ignored it and continued the single-handed fight until his ammunition was exhausted. He then made his way to his company, refused medical attention, and organized the company in a counterattack which forced the Germans to withdraw. His directing of artillery fire wiped out many of the enemy; he killed or wounded about 50. 2d Lt. Murphy's indomitable courage and his refusal to give an inch of ground saved his company from possible encirclement and destruction, and enabled it to hold the woods which had been the enemy's objective.

Murphy. Answered the voice on the phone: "Who's Audie Murphy?" The major networks gave only a few minutes of their evening news to his death, and when the Old Guard laid him to rest at Arlington National Cemetery, two of the three networks ignored it.

Imagine that. Ignoring, or worse, forgetting Audie Murphy. These men deserve to be remembered, and their stories must be passed to our children. Andrew Jackson urged the boys of his day to study and emulate the Scottish chiefs. He was right, and our children should add men such as Murphy to learn that a man's outward size isn't as important as the size of his heart, that fear must be subdued not accommodated, and that a real man sometimes must stand and fight. Men such as Murphy aren't merely born, they are made. And what makes them is the cultural milieu in which they are raised. When Murphy was a boy, our society treasured manly integrity and courage. It held up a man willing to use fists or firearms, when necessary, as heroic. It did not cavil at violence the way we wrongly exploit the term now; it did not expect a bully patrol manned by little girls to protect little boys on the playground. It expected boys to act like boys, to grow up to be men, real men, the kind of man Murphy became. So we must remember Audie Murphy. At our peril, we forget him and those like him whose "name and fame"—to borrow Douglas MacArthur's words in praise of the American fighting man—"are the birthright of every American citizen . . . [who] has written his own history and written it in red on his enemy's breast."

Without these men, we have no history and no heroes for our sons. We have nothing but the pumped-up celluloid pa-lookas of the MTV generation.

8

David Crockett

Be always sure you are right, then go ahead.

—*David Crockett*

When David Crockett lost his bid for reelection to the U.S. Congress in 1835, he gathered with friends for drinks at the Union Hotel in Memphis, Tennessee. Supporters called upon the canebrake congressman for a few words. "Since you have chosen to elect a man with a timber toe to succeed me," Crockett famously said, "you may all go to hell and I will go to Texas."

Crockett departed the next day. "He wore that same veritable coon skin cap and hunting shirt, bearing upon his shoulder his ever-faithful rifle," a young admirer remembered. The King of the Wild Frontier carried no other equipment "save his shot pouch and powder-horn" and set himself upon the fateful trail to enduring legend. Destination: the Alamo.

In Walt Disney's version, Crockett is one of the last men standing, swinging his musket at the surging, relentless Mexican horde. In John Wayne's film, Crockett takes a lance in the heart and detonates a gunpowder magazine. Was he one of the first killed or among the last? We don't know. Dubious accounts put a quaking Crockett hiding in a pickle barrel or otherwise captured and executed.

The latter stories are unlikely, contrary to Crockett's character. He told tall tales, liked a good joke, and pulled a friend's leg. But no coward was he. Crockett died a hero; historians say little else. He fought to the end with the Alamo's 187 valiant defenders led by Col. William Travis and Jim Bowie. "Too much has been made over the details of how David died at the Alamo," wrote biographer James Shackford. "Such details are not important. What is important is that he died as he had lived."

How Crockett lived. He defended the meek and put-upon penurious and was a principled, self-made, largely self-educated gentlemen of courage. Thanks to his biographers and Walt Disney, he became the transcendent icon of the frontier American, and many of Crockett's genuine deeds are lost amid the welter of legend and myth. Yet stripping away the latter, we discover the truth that he was every bit the grandiose figure one would suspect he was, and had to have been, to have dominated the American stage.

Early Life and Childhood

He was born in Greene County, Tennessee, on the Nolichucky River on August 17, 1786. Creek and Cherokee Indians massacred his grandparents, Scots-Irish who came to Tennessee through Virginia's Shenandoah Valley. Like Andrew Jackson's early life, Crockett's was brutal, as it was for many youngsters in the untamed frontier of America. More than that, his father was a heavy tippler who used hickory rod to impose stern discipline. Describing his childhood in today's terms, we would say Crockett's violent father emotionally and physically abused the boy. Regardless, boyhood experiences made the man.

When David turned twelve years old, his father hired him out to a wagoner driving cattle to Natural Bridge, Virginia, in the Shenandoah Valley. For the lad's work, wagoner Jacob Siler would pay the father. It was a 225-mile passage, and Crockett returned home alone. He traversed wild country, streams, knee-deep mires, and drenching, chilling rains, eating wild game off the land. Siler wanted to retain the boy, but young Crockett refused and made plans with some passing travelers for a nocturnal escape. Amid the dark and gloom of night, with the wind howling through the trees, the wayward lad trudged seven miles in knee-deep snow until he reached the saviors who promised to help him home. He arrived in late 1798 or early 1799.

About the same time, schoolmaster Benjamin Kitchen alighted in the Crocketts' rustic milieu, and young David landed in his classroom. After just four days in school and barely learning his ABCs, he ran afoul of a bully. "Fierce and reckless as a catamount," hagiographer John Abbott reported, Crockett decided to thrash the ruffian away from the school and the eyes of Kitchen, lest the schoolmaster stop the hand of justice. Crockett sprang upon his foe like a "panther," and "with tooth and nail he assailed him, biting, scratching, pounding, until the boy cried for mercy." Having bested the bully, Crockett had to face the wrath of either his father or the schoolmaster. So Crockett refused to return to the school and hid in the woods. Kitchen discovered the ruse and told John Crockett, who was in no mood for the young scholar's clandestine but justifiable shenanigans. When the drunken patriarch ordered his son's return to school and a certain caning, David refused. There ensued a mile-long chase into the backwoods, with the elder Crockett wielding a two-year-old hickory stick. The boy escaped, this time for years.

Crockett earned four dollars by helping to drive a herd through Charlottesville then to Front Royal, Virginia, 375 miles from home. On his return home, he joined wagoner Adam Myers, who was driving cattle to Gerardstown below Winchester. This job done, Myers could not find work taking a herd back to Tennessee, as Myers had agreed with Crockett, and instead made trips to Alexandria. Crockett was homesick, but "when I thought . . . of Kitchen . . . and of the race with my father, and of the big hickory stick he carried, and of the fierceness of the storm of wrath I had left him in, I was afraid to venture back. . . . The promised whipping came slap down upon every thought of home." So Crockett stayed in Gerardstown, working for twenty-five cents per day until he earned a king's ransom of seven dollars.

In 1800, Myers and Crockett traveled to Baltimore, where David became enamored of the wharves and sailing ships and dreamed of a trip to London. A sea captain sought David's employ when the lad visited his ship. Crockett had given his meager wages to Myers for safekeeping, and when he announced his plans to leave, he again faced the specter of a whipping, this time from a man with no legal or moral claim to his loyalty or obedience. Myers refused to return the boy's small purse, so Crockett fled for home penniless, with nothing but the tattered clothes on this back. On this journey, he encountered wagoner Henry Myers. Listening to Crockett's lachrymose tale of thievery, he promised to reclaim the ill-gotten booty. But by the time the two Myers met, nothing was left to claim; the money was spent. News of the larceny spread, and sympathetic men collected money to send the boy home. In the end, Crockett had three dollars and two feet to carry him.

Along the way, Crockett worked for a hatter who went broke and found his pockets empty after eighteen months of work. He took up odd jobs after that, eventually earning enough to set off again. This time a more perilous adventure awaited. He crossed the roiling New River, whipped into waves by chilling winds that left his clothes nearly frozen. Undaunted, Crockett walked three miles until he found a home and implored the occupants to let him warm by the fire. Soon he was afoot again, hiking ninety miles to an uncle's home, where he stayed for a few weeks.

On returning home, Crockett was six feet tall and nearly sixteen. Even though John Crockett rejoiced to have his son home, he said that David owed him a final service. Ever obedient to the unwritten law that a father owned his son's labor, David agreed to work for another man, Abraham Wilson, to whom his father owed thirty-six dollars. Finished that term, Crockett thought himself free, and needing new accouterments, worked for an honest Quaker from North Carolina, John Kennedy. Unhappily, Kennedy was a creditor as well; John Crockett owed him forty dollars, a debt David felt obliged to relieve. After six months gratis labor, Crockett returned to his father with Kennedy's note. John thought Kennedy sent the bill for collection, and knowing he couldn't pay it, offered excuses to David. But the ever-faithful son explained that the note was a gift, a bill paid in full. John Crockett "shed a heap of tears," recalled David, but the note, biographer William C. Davis writes, wasn't a gift: "It was his declaration of independence."

INDIAN FIGHTER AND SCOUT

WE OF the early twenty-first century who think "independence" means getting a driver's license, with our silly notions of "adolescence" and myriad pathologies from pimples to puppy love, from depression to bullying, can only wonder at men such as Crockett. His rough youth on the frontier was notable for its material and financial deprivation. David Crockett had nothing. Like Audie Murphy, while being fun-loving, he never sat about having "fun." Surviving was a full-time endeavor.

And survive he did. Other than the four days as a youngster in Kitchen's canebrake classroom, Crockett received just about one hundred days of schooling and learned to read when he was about eighteen. Like many of his kind, Crockett's prowess with his flintlock was frontier lore. One tale attests to his marksmanship. The backwoodsmen held shooting contests; twenty-five cents for a shot at a target to win a quarter of beef. A few days before his proposed marriage to a Margaret Elder, an engagement that ended, Crockett entered a contest. He won all four quarters, the whole beef.

Crockett eventually married Polly Finley, who bore him two sons. But in just a few years, war against the Creek Indians beckoned. The tribe had slaughtered five hundred white settlers at Fort Mims, Alabama, and although Crockett, Davis writes, was "too cheerful, too even-tempered" to want to fight and preferred "fun to feuding. . . . [S]elf defense was something else." Perhaps harkening back to his grandparents' murder, and considering the possibility of his own family's massacre, Crockett enlisted. "My dander was up," he wrote to Polly, "and nothing but war could bring it right again."

With the Tennessee Volunteer Mounted Rifleman in November 1813, Crockett joined in the retaliatory raid known as the battle of Tallusahatchee. There, the volunteers stormed a Creek Indian settlement. The Creeks fought "with savage fury," Brig. Gen. John Coffee wrote later, "and met death with all its horrors without shrinking or complaining: not one asked to be spared." They were no match for the enraged

Americans. "We shot them like dogs," Crockett remembered, and he helped shoot down a squaw who felled a militiaman with a bow and arrow. She "had at least twenty balls blown through her," he noted. The warriors, about two hundred in the village, "fought as long as they could stand or sit," to finish Coffee's rendition of the battle. For the Americans, vengeance for the massacre at Fort Mims, and perhaps for Crockett's own grandparents, was the order of the day. Forty warriors were burned alive in a wooden house. The next day, the men ate potatoes stored in the cellar of that house; "hunger compelled us to eat them, though I had a little rather not," he wrote. "The oil of the Indians we had burned up on the day before had run down on them, they looked like they had been stewed with fat meat."

The intensity of their hunger demonstrates the deprivations of the men who fought in the Creek War, and explains why Andrew Jackson faced more than one mutiny. Napoleon said that an army travels on its stomach; Jackson's men were starving.

A week later, the volunteers fought at Talladega, facing a thousand Creeks who surged at the Americans like a "cloud of Egyptian locusts, and screaming like all the young devils had been turned loose, with the old devil of it all at their head." Though Crockett did not serve in the decisive battles at Emuckfau or Enotachopco creeks or Horseshoe Bend, his service was nonetheless faithful; he volunteered, served as scout for his unit, and went to battle fearlessly. It simply isn't true that Crockett participated in a one-sided massacre of the Creeks at Tallusahatchee. The Creeks were ready for battle, and even the women were fighting. The squaw who went down in a hail of gunfire could have easily put an arrow into Crockett as any other man.

After the war, Crockett returned home and began a public

LIBRARY OF CONGRESS

David Crockett was a frontiersman, entrepreneur, congressman, bear hunter, and warrior. He left home a twelve-year-old boy and traveled through wild, frontier Virginia and Tennessee. He returned a man. An audacious hunter, he killed more than a hundred bears in a single season. He even killed a bear with a knife.

life in 1821, at age thirty-five, with election to the Tennessee General Assembly. Though Crockett turned to politics, he never lost his familiarity with the woods and canebrakes that whelped him. He was still a hunter and in one season felled more than a hundred bears with a hunting party. He killed a bruin at night with a long knife, having trapped the beast, with the aid of his dogs, in a crevice. In the 1820s, Crockett was proprietor of a barrel-stave enterprise, taking sail to New Orleans down the Obion River and the Mighty Mississippi. But the great muddy was a different river of fish than the placid Obion. It was fast flowing, wide, and unmanageable in two flatboats that Crockett and his men had joined together. Instead of being more manageable, the two joined boats were more dangerous.

One day, a few hours before sunrise, as they approached Memphis, Crockett was inside the cabin resting, when a sawyer—a felled tree emerging from the water—split the two crafts and drove Crockett's boat into a piece of driftwood. The current pushed Crockett's craft under the woody flotsam, trapping him in the cabin as the water rushed in. He yelled for help, and his fellow boatmen pulled him out, stripping him of his clothes and some flesh; he "was literally skinn'd like a rabbit."

Politics, which next found him in Congress, had not softened him.

CROCKETT IN THE CONGRESS

CROCKETT'S OPPOSITION to Andrew Jackson's Indian removal bill is a matter of some renown, even if his opposition seems odd in juxtaposition to the Creek War, the prejudices of the era, and the Creeks' murder of his grandparents. The bill would have forcibly moved peaceful Indians in Mississippi, Alabama, Tennessee, and Georgia to a territory west of the Mississippi River. Crockett's resistance to the measure pitted him not only against Jackson but also his constituents, and though he never gave a speech on the floor of the House to oppose it, he voted against it. As William C. Davis noted, it would have given the president unfettered use of five hundred thousand dollars, and Crockett clearly calculated on winning favor in the Whig Party:

> [Yet Crockett] also seems to have felt some genuine sympathy for the plight of the Indians. After all, he knew their situation: poor, despised, friendless, and now to be landless. . . . [W]hile he undoubtedly entertained all the prejudices of his time and place, he could never fail to empathize with anyone who was poor, downtrodden and helpless. That was in the

simple generosity of his nature, one of those kinder elements that led so many to see in him a "natural gentleman." Ever the egalitarian, David refused to countenance that one class enjoyed more entitlement than another.

Such feelings also fomented his desire to abolish the military academy at West Point. He argued that the poor paid taxes to provide a free education for those of privilege and high social station; that is, "to pick the pockets of the poor to educate the sons of the rich."

But perhaps Crockett never articulated his principles so eloquently or forcefully as in his speech against a bill to appropriate ten thousand dollars for the relief of naval war hero Stephen Decatur's widow. Only a hard heart would vote against such a stipend, many would believe, but Crockett had good reasons. "Mr. Speaker," he began,

> We must not permit our respect for the dead or our sympathy for a part of the living to lead us into an act of injustice to the balance of the living. . . . Congress has no power to appropriate this money as an act of charity. Every member upon this floor knows it. We have the right, as individuals, to give away as much of our own money as we please in charity; but . . . we have no right so to appropriate a dollar of the public money.
>
> . . .
>
> Mr. Speaker, the deceased lived long after the close of the war; he was in office to the day of his death, and I have never heard that the government was in arrears to him. This government can owe no debts but for services rendered, and at a stipulated price. If it is a debt, how much is it . . . ? If it is a debt, we owe more than we can ever hope to pay, for we owe the widow of every soldier who fought in the War of 1812 precisely the same amount. There is a woman in my neighbor-

hood, the widow of as gallant a man as ever shouldered a musket. . . . [B]ut if I were to introduce a bill to appropriate five or ten thousand dollars for her benefit, I should be laughed at, and my bill would not get five votes in this House. There are thousands of widows in the country just such [as this] one. . . .

Sir, this is no debt. The government did not owe it to the deceased when he was alive; it could not contract it after he died. I do not wish to be rude, but I must be plain. . . . We cannot, without the grossest corruption, appropriate this money as the payment of a debt. We have not the semblance of authority to appropriate it as a charity. . . . I am the poorest man on this floor. I cannot vote for this bill, but I will give one week's pay to the object, and if every member of Congress will do the same, it will amount to more than the bill asks.

Hard cases, Crockett knew, make bad law, and although the widow's relief bill was defeated, his principles and practical wisdom did not help reelect him in 1835. Taking his leave from the Potomac, he famously proclaimed his impending argosy to Texas.

The Alamo, the Legend, the Man

THE ALAMO forever engraved Crockett in the American psyche. He went to explore Texas, to roam its indescribable vastness, and not incidentally, to begin a new political career. Although he didn't intend to fight, he volunteered for military service and took an oath to the new government, insisting it contain the word *republican*. He landed at the Alamo in early February 1836.

The rest, as they say, is history. "The real courage" at the Alamo, Davis wrote, "lay in the fact that for nearly two weeks,

Travis, Crockett and Bowie and the rest knowingly placed and kept themselves in harm's way, aware each day that the Mexicans could overwhelm them at the next dawn, and yet they stayed." Overwhelmed and facing certain death, Travis established Crockett's valor in his famous missive of February 25 to Sam Houston: "The Hon. David Crockett was seen at all points, animating the men to do their duty."

Before sunrise on March 6, some eighteen hundred of Santa Anna's soldiers stormed the compound. "Come on boys, the Mexicans are upon us, and we'll give them Hell," Travis yelled at the north wall, blasting Mexicans with his double-barreled shotgun as they scaled the ramparts. From below, a three-quarter-inch ball struck Travis in the forehead, killing him instantly. Mexicans burst into Bowie's room, and discovering him under a blanket, febrile and delirious with typhoid, they killed him.

The details of Crockett's death are murky. James Atkins Shackford avers it was "quite undramatic; that he was one of the first to fall, and he died unarmed." Perhaps. Other scholarship based upon a Mexican officer's account, reputed to be a forgery and featured in the 2004 film *The Alamo,* has Crockett captured and executed. Davis noted that he could have been "killed by a cannon's blast and a rush of bayonets. . . . No one who knew him saw him fall and lived to tell of it."

However Crockett died, he died like a real man, and that notwithstanding, others knew him before he fell and did live to tell about it. They tell the story of a boy and man who, like Andrew Jackson, stands in stark contrast to the modern adolescent and preening popinjays we call men. Again, men such as Crockett aren't simply born. They are made, and those of us who have never seen a moment of privation or strife are made of lesser stuff. In a sense, we are incomplete. Crockett's is a story of unimaginable Herculean strife. At a tender age, for nearly four years, he slogged through the rustic leagues of back country and woods through Tennessee and Virginia, over streams and raging rivers, through knee-deep snow, to return home a man. He survived malaria. With just six months of formal education, he shaped national policy in Congress and more firmly grasped the federal Constitution than the degreed lawyers and politicians who today misappropriate funds with pork-barreling larceny and brazen bribery disguised as "constituent service."

"[Crockett's] life was one of indomitable bravery," to finish Shackford's fitting encomium. "His death was a death of intrepid courage. His life was one of whole hearted dedication to his own concepts of liberty. He died staking his life against what he regarded as intolerable tyranny."

Crockett was killed at the Alamo in 1836 with the rest of its valiant defenders; they fought to the last man. Though the details of Crockett's death are uncertain, there is no question he died a hero. After all, he could have left the Alamo at any time. "Be always sure you are right," he said, "then go ahead."

9

Andrew Jackson

One man with courage makes a majority.

—*Andrew Jackson*

IT WAS JANUARY 30, 1835. President Andrew Jackson was sixty-eight years old, his body battered from years of rough living: captivity during the Revolution, smallpox, gunshot wounds in duels, and twenty years duty in the Indian wars. He suffered dysentery, rheumatism, amyloidosis, and stood stalwartly amid the deadly arrows and bullets at Horseshoe Bend. Though frail, Jackson was still the feisty gamecock of his early days.

That chilly day, Jackson attended the funeral of Rep. Warren Davis at the Capitol. Various accounts put the services in the House chamber or the rotunda, where presidents lie in state. Wherever the services were, Jackson was emerging from the defining edifice of our republic when Richard Lawrence, a deranged house painter, accosted him. Lawrence pulled a derringer and fired at the president. Undaunted, Old Hickory raised his walking stick and charged his assailant. Lawrence produced another pistol. Another misfire. The odds? One in 250,000.

Lawrence, who thought he was heir to the British throne and that Jackson owed him money, lived out his days in an asylum, but the more interesting and telling figure in this story is Jackson. Had the fracas continued, Jackson would likely have beaten the man senseless, if not killed him. This is but one example of the fearlessness of our seventh president.

To understand this mythic figure, one must plow into the glebe of the American frontier. There, the past became prologue. Jackson was whelped in the Waxhaws, the rustic border country between the Carolina colonies where the Jackson clan landed in 1765. They were Ulster Scots, the hardy clansmen who settled in Ireland then fled that country for America to seek prosperity and a better life.

The American Scots-Irish of Jackson's day were cut from the rough cloth of the Celtic clans. Intensely loyal, they were ever ready to fight, particularly in a blood feud, over land or their women or for simple honor. Their fearlessness in battle is the stuff of both legend and fact, so insight into Jackson is to be gained from learning about the Scots. They were men such as William Wallace, the brawny, six-foot-six-inch thirteenth-century warrior who avenged his father's murder by killing the guilty English knight, then avenged his wife's murder by killing the guilty sheriff of Lanark. A rebellion began, and in 1297, Wallace led his warriors to kill five thousand English at the battle of Stirling Bridge. The English later captured and hanged him until he was nearly dead. He was drawn (intestines removed and burned) and quartered, and his remains were scattered countrywide. His head landed on a pike at London Bridge.

Jackson said that young men should study these "Scottish chiefs," that a boy could find no better example of manly character than Wallace. He was "the best model for a young man," Jackson taught. "We find in him the truly undaunted courage, always ready to brave any danger, for the relief of his country or his friend." But Jackson's admiration of these men is unsurprising. He was hewn from the same stand of Celtic oak as Robert the Bruce, the warrior-king who, in 1314, commanded the Argyles at Bannockburn and slew thirty thousand English. Jackson's mother descended from the Bruce.

A Teenage POW

Blessed with these cultural roots and genes, Jackson was born on March 15, 1767. Like many boys of his time, he began life with misfortune. His father died before Jackson was born, but happily, providence gave him a strong, principled mother, Elizabeth. From the start, he was a "fighting cock," as one biographer called him. As with most frontier boys, Jackson's play included much foot racing and wrestling. "I could throw him three times out of four," an older bigger boy said, but he "would never stay throwed." And Jackson was not a boy to brook an insult. Some boys once packed a muzzleloader full of powder and dared him to fire it, hoping the recoil would throw him to the ground. The young "fighting cock" picked up the weapon and fired. The discharge sent him reeling. "By God," he said, "if one of you laughs, I'll kill him."

The British offered the first test of Jackson's courage. He was just a boy, thirteen or so, when three hundred British cavalry under Lt. Col. Banastre Tarleton massacred a detachment of soldiers in the Waxhaw. To avenge the death of his brother Hugh after the battle at Stono Ferry, Andrew and his brother Robert joined the Revolution by helping their mother tend the wounded. From the moment the British invested the Waxhaw country, Jackson was in the thick of it. He was a courier at the battle of Hanging Rock and fought with the Carolina patriots. He watched men fall at his side, yet he had barely attained what we now call adolescence.

Jackson's Revolutionary War exploits include one of the most heralded acts of his illustrious career when he and his brother were captured. In captivity, a British officer demanded that Jackson, not yet fifteen, shine his boots. The Waxhaw boy defied his imperial captor.

"Sir, I am a prisoner of war and claim to be treated as such."

Unsurprisingly, the Redcoat didn't cotton to the impertinent insubordination of the stripling and brought his cutlass down at the boy's head. The lad threw up his left hand to deflect the blow, but the blade cut deep, right to the bone of his fingers. The blade also cut his head to his skull. The officer demanded the same of Robert, who also refused and suffered a severe blow to the head.

The Jackson boys next endured a forty-mile, two-day march and then time in a British prison, where the prisoners, barely fed, suffered egregious, oozing wounds. The jail was redolent of human waste and, worse, some prisoners had smallpox. The Jacksons were eventually released to the custody of their mother in a prisoner exchange, but the boys left the tender mercies of their captors with more than a scar. Like other prisoners, they contracted smallpox. This too young Andrew survived, his mother nursing him back to health after a forty-five-mile march back home, barefoot and without a coat. His brother Robert died.

Soon afterward, tending to American prisoners, Elizabeth contracted typhus and died. Her parting words before leaving for this grim, nursing duty included, "Never sue for slander. Settle them cases yourself." As Jackson recalled it, never sue for "insult or battery or defamation. The law affords no rem-

Andrew Jackson lost his family during the American Revolution and was himself, at the age of fourteen, imprisoned by the British. But these hardships did not stop him. He became a lawyer and eventually led militia forces against raiding Indians and the invading British during the War of 1812.

edy for such outrage that can satisfy a gentleman. Fight." It was advice he carried for the rest of his life.

In 1781, fourteen-year-old Andrew Jackson was a battle-scarred veteran of the Revolutionary War and an orphan. Most of us can hardly imagine losing one parent at age fourteen, much less a widowed mother and two brothers, or fighting in a war in which the nation's independence hung in the balance.

Jackson did all of it.

BRAVE MAN

HAVING SURVIVED the war, smallpox, and the death of his family, seventeen-year-old Andrew Jackson began studying law. He was an intimidating, domineering man, the alpha male in any group of stags. No one slighted Jackson and got away with it. He never threatened or cursed. The mere glare from his icy blue eyes was enough to stop a man cold, and as biographer Robert V. Remini described many a harrowing brush with death, Jackson's audacity and nerve served him well, frightening foes and flabbergasting friends.

Early in Jackson's law career, a man he described as a "big bullying fellow" stepped on his toes to pick a fight. Gentlemen didn't resort to fisticuffs, but Jackson's social station was such that he could not challenge the ruffian to pistol shots. So Jackson picked up a fence rail and jammed the end "full in his belly." The blow "doubled him up," he remembered, and when the miscreant went down to the ground, "I stamped on him." When the enraged opponent got to his feet, he "was about to fly at me like a tiger," but "he gave me one look, Sir, and turned away, frightened, a whipped man and feeling like one."

One of Jackson's closest encounters with the grim reaper came in a duel with Charles Dickenson, described as an "affluent dandy," a drinker, and the best shot in Tennessee. Dickenson insulted the honor of Rachel, Jackson's wife, a peccancy for which Jackson confronted the offender. Dickenson apologized, citing his inebriation, and Jackson let the insult pass. But Dickenson did not leave well enough alone. The feud between the two also involved a bet over a horse race and a middleman named Swann, who insulted Jackson and wound up on the business end of Jackson's cane in a tavern. Jackson would have shot him if he had been armed; Swann fled the scene. Dickenson posted a letter to Jackson, claiming that Swann's remarks about Jackson were true, and the verbal fratch eventually escalated to published articles in the *Nashville Review* newspaper. In those columns, Dickenson called him a "worthless poltroon and coward" who would avoid "the field of honor." In those days in the South, that meant facing a man according to the code duello, which called for pistol shots at a prescribed time and place.

"I hope, sir," Jackson replied in writing, "your courage will be ample security to me that I will obtain speedily that satisfaction due for the insults offered." Thus did Jackson issue the challenge.

On the way to the May 30, 1806, duel at Harrison's Mill on the Red River in Kentucky's Logan County, Dickenson stopped along the road to demonstrate his marksmanship by cutting hung pieces of string at twenty-four feet, the distance at which he would face Jackson. He left one at a tavern along the road and told the proprietor, "If General Jackson comes along this road, show him that!"

Jackson determined that the only way to beat Dickenson was to let his foe shoot first and hope the lead ball didn't kill him. He knew Dickenson wouldn't miss. When the moment came, Jackson's second, Maj. John Overton, called for the men to fire. Dickenson shot first. His ball thudded into Jackson's chest, breaking two ribs and lodging there. The future president, left arm clutching his chest, stood tall. Dickenson stepped back. "Great God," he exclaimed. "Have I missed him?"

"Back to the mark, sir," Overton ordered. Aiming his pistol at Dickenson, Jackson pulled the trigger, but the hammer stopped halfway toward the pad. The seconds conferred and agreed the duel could continue. Jackson recocked and fired. The shot ripped through Dickenson and out his back. The best shot in Tennessee bled to death.

Seeing Jackson's wound, Overton exclaimed, "My God! General Jackson, are you hit?"

"Oh! I believe that he has pinked me a little," Jackson coolly replied. "Let's look at it. But say nothing about it there."

Vastly outnumbered, Jackson defeated the British at New Orleans in 1814. The stunning victory made him a national hero for the rest of his life. U.S. fortunes suffered greatly in the War of 1812—the capital was in ruins and the army had not won a single battle—but Jackson's victory restored the nation's confidence in itself.

Jackson didn't want the dying Dickenson to know he had been hit. And nearly fatally so.

In 1813, brothers Jesse and Thomas Hart Benton ambushed Jackson in a tavern in Nashville, with the ensuing gunfight leaving him in ever more dire straits than the first. Jackson was caning Thomas Hart when Jesse Benton put two balls into Jackson's left arm and shoulder, leaving the appendage useless for some time. But the wounds did not keep Old Hickory down. Not fully recovered and nearly unable to ride, Jackson rose from his sickbed to command the army that went south to fight the Red Stick Creeks. His health was such that he was tied into the saddle with wooden poles. Though ill, Jackson's Celtic blood was up, and he prepared himself to fight. He did, gloriously, but not before a group of his men threatened to desert Fort Strother after an engagement at Talladega, Alabama.

The men had run out of supplies. They were hungry, tired, and ready to go home, but no more down on their luck than Jackson, who was not only starving but also suffering dysentery. Eventually, the men were fed, but a company of volunteers tried to move off toward home. Jackson mounted his steed and rode ahead. He threatened to kill any man who deserted. "A shaft of implacable determination stretched high in the saddle of his horse," biographer Remini wrote, "eyes flashing, grizzled hair bristling on his forehead. . . . To brave this fury was madness."

When Jackson returned to the main body of his army, a brigade prepared to desert. Jackson grabbed a musket and, using his right arm, rested it over the neck of his horse. The men knew he would shoot, and no wonder they dubbed him "Old Hickory," watching him march with the troops and fight alongside them. Now, he stood prepared to kill the first one who moved. The general put down another rebellion by the sheer force of his will. Wrote one of his officers, "He is represented as a tyrant & a despot. Never was there a milder man, when mildness could possibly succeed—never a more energetic one, when energy was necessary; but at all times never did a general love his army so much or labour so much to promote their interest."

In his engagement against the Red Sticks at Horseshoe Bend in 1814, Jackson commanded the battlefield. "Charge!" he yelled when his men attacked the Indians' barricade at the bend. Although a man ignorant of the plain at West Point and the academic science of warfare, he was, in the words of one observer, "firm and energetic, and at the same time perfectly self-possessed, his example and his authority alike contributed to arrest the flying, and give confidence to those who maintained their ground. . . . In the midst of a shower of balls, of which he seemed unmindful, he was seen . . . rallying the alarmed, halting them in their flight, forming his columns and inspiriting them by his example."

Certainly, Jackson killed many Indians, one reason they dubbed him "Sharp Knife." Still, he was no murderous butcher. One of the captives taken in the first engagement of the Creek War at the battle of Tallahusatchee was an infant, about ten months old, named Lyncoya. The Indian women were about to murder the boy because his parents were dead, but the troops stopped them and delivered the boy to Jackson. The man who would shoot another dead for insulting his wife took the infant to his tent and fed him brown sugar and water. Jackson sent the boy to the Hermitage, his home in Nashville, and gave him his name and an education.

In January 1815, Jackson led three thousand Americans to defeat twice as many British at the battle of New Orleans. The British suffered two thousand casualties, including top commanders, to the Americans' thirteen killed, thirty-nine wounded, and nineteen missing. Jackson's heroic stand at the Crescent City set his path to the White House in 1828. When the madman Lawrence pulled his derringer and fired, the old warbird was still full of fight.

Throughout his career, Jackson doubtless made enemies. But they respected him, and some became friends. Senator Thomas Hart Benton, who conspired with his brother to kill Jackson in ambush, became one of his strongest supporters.

In Death

JACKSON SPENT his waning years in immense pain and ill health. Writes essayist Bertram Wyatt Brown: "The former

President's health was so poor that his will to survive, about which all his biographers marvel, resists credibility. If heroism were defined by a defiance of pain alone, Jackson was by far the most heroic of all the American presidents."

In 1845, the seventy-eight-year-old Jackson died quietly and with dignity, his black servants and slaves, as biographer Arthur Schlesinger recorded, gathered around his deathbed. "Do not cry," he told the wailing mourners. "I shall meet you in heaven, yes, I hope to meet you all in heaven white and black. Why should you weep?" Old Hickory asked, looking around his room. "I am in the hands of the Lord! who is about to relieve me, you should rejoice, not weep!"

You don't weep for a man such as Jackson. You celebrate

If Jackson was known for anything beside his outstanding presidency, during which he opposed rechartering the unconstitutional Bank of the United States and refused to obey an edict from Chief Justice John Marshall, it was his astounding physical courage, particularly in withstanding debilitating pain.

him and honor his example by emulating his valor. But what made Andrew Jackson a fearless man? Without doubt, genes were partly responsible. And so did his cultural inheritance from the stout Ulster Scots who settled the Waxhaws, that hardy band descended from Wallace and Bruce.

So also did the frontier in which Jackson and other boys of his era were reared, in woods among Indians and wild animals, where life could be extinguished not only by disease but also by a raging beast a few paces away from the cabin door. Boys of Jackson's era did not play computer games. They raced, likely barefoot, over the hard ground. They wrestled. They hunted in the woods for game.

Jackson's conception of manhood was rooted in the men

This is one of the earliest photographs of a U.S. president, though technically it is a daguerreotype, and Jackson had left the White House eight years earlier (though he had tremendous national influence for the rest of his life). The image was captured shortly before Jackson's death in 1845 at his home, the Hermitage, in Nashville.

he admired as a boy, the tales of heroism that demonstrated how a man of honor and valor behaves not only toward other men but also toward women. Jackson was deferential toward and solicitous of the latter, but he dominated and terrified the former . . . if they got on his wrong side.

Today's men and boys are on the wrong side. The face of the country changes little by little, the fictional Homer Bannon said, because of the men we admire. Jackson knew this, which was why he suggested that young boys study the Scottish chiefs: William Wallace and Robert the Bruce. So Jackson taught others not only to behave like real men but also what men are worth study. He told us, in so many words, "These are the men you should admire. These are the men you should follow."

Jackson, one of our greatest presidents, a descendent of the Scottish chiefs himself, was one of them. The indomitable courage demonstrated throughout his life—in youth against the British, in young manhood at Harrison's Mill, in middle age at Horseshoe Bend, and as an old man at the Capitol—are testaments to Jackson's impavid indifference to mortal peril and his conception of manly rectitude. They made Jackson what he was, and they ensure his eternal, mythic place in American history.

10

Robert E. Lee

I did not know then . . . that he was absolutely
stainless in his private life. I did not know then, as I do
now, that he had been a model youth and young man;
but I had before me the most manly and entire
gentlemen I ever saw.

—*Alexander H. Stephens*

ROBERT E. LEE WAS so grand a figure, so dissimilar to any American considered a hero today, or even when he lived and before, that measuring a man against him is almost unfair. Yet Lee is the standard against which any man should measure himself.

Harry Crocker, author of *Robert E. Lee on Leadership*, explained Lee's example. When life presents us with a question, great or small, we might find the answer by asking a simple question: "What would Lee do?" If anyone wants to evaluate his actions, he can ask, simply, "What would Lee have done?"

Lee was a Christian gentleman, a cavalier of the old order, the embodiment of chivalry. He was physically and morally courageous, humble, loyal, and steadfast in his Christian faith. He carried his cross. For Lee, duty was all; sacrifice, self-denial, and self-discipline were the eleventh, twelfth, and thirteenth commandments; prayer, a daily debt joyfully paid to a merciful, beneficent, and loving God. As one writer described it, many Southerners who worship at the shrine of Lee would portray him as St. George, slaying the Yankee dragon. Yet he was also akin to St. Francis: loving, kind to man and beast alike, retiring, an apostle of humility. Lee never thought of himself before others; he always came fourth—after God, family, and friends. He did not exalt himself, and after the war for Southern independence, he rarely discussed his role in it and he wrote nothing about it.

War won renown for Lee, but the impeccable whole of his manhood is our model.

BOYHOOD AND MEXICO

HE WAS born January 19, 1807, at Stratford Hall, the ancestral manse in Virginia's Northern Neck, the mortar of its bricks having been mixed through seven centuries. To understand the man, one must understand his ancestry and his own model of manhood: George Washington.

During the Norman conquest of Britain, the family's founder, Lancelot de Lee, courageously fought with William the Conqueror at the battle of Hastings in 1066. Another of Lee's ancestor's was Lionel Lee, who fought with Richard the Lionhearted in the Third Crusade. The Lees who came to the colonies sired brothers Richard Henry, Francis Lightfoot, and Arthur Lee. On June 7, 1776, in the Continental Congress, Richard Henry offered the motion for independence from Great Britain, seconded by his fast friend John Adams. Richard and Francis signed the Declaration of Independence; Arthur was an emissary to France during the Revolution. Robert E. Lee's father was Lighthorse Harry Lee, George Washington's intrepid cavalry commander who, fighting alongside Francis Marion, "the Swamp Fox," drove the British from South Carolina. His mother was Ann Carter Lee, the daughter of another of Virginia's first families. Maternally, one historical account noted, and like Andrew Jackson, Lee's ancestry traced to Robert the Bruce; he may have been descended from three other Scottish warriors who fought the English at Bannockburn in 1314. Thus was Lee's pedigree firmly grafted not only to the infant tree of American liberty but also to the taproot of Western civilization.

From early childhood, Lee's hero was George Washington, his father's commander and the first president of the United States. "The family held fast to this reverence," biographer Douglas Southall Freeman wrote. "In the home where Robert was trained, God came first, and then Washington." Indeed, when Lee married Mary Custis, Washington's granddaughter by adoption, "he married Arlington," the home of Washington's adopted son and Martha Washington's grandson, George Washington Parke Custis, which overlooked Washington City from the heights above the Potomac River. For much of his adult life from young manhood, Washington's relics surrounded Lee and would ever provide the inspiration for his conduct as a gentlemen, soldier, and American. "The marriage," Freeman quotes another biographer and relative, "in the eyes of the world made Robert Lee the representative of the family of the founder of American liberty."

Freeman continued:

> The Father of his country was no mere historical figure to him, great but impersonal and indistinct. . . . Washington was as real to him as if the majestic Virginian had stepped down nightly from the canvas at Arlington and had talked reminiscently with the family about the birth of an earlier revolution. Daily for almost thirty years, whenever Lee had been at home, his environment had been a constant suggestion of the same ideal. He had come to view duty as Washington did, to act as

he thought Washington would, even perhaps, to emulate the grave self-contained courtesy of the great American rebel.

Thus did Lee's aristocratic genealogy, family and cultural heritage, his indissoluble bond to the early republic and to Great Britain before that set the unwavering course for his life.

God handed Lee a terrible blow at an early age. His debt-ridden father abandoned the family to roam the Caribbean, then he died in 1818, when Robert was just eleven, on Cumberland Island, off the Georgia coast. Lighthorse Harry left the family in debt, but with the firm guidance of Ann, his son was imbued with the virtues that would see him through West Point and across the battlefields of Mexico and the War Between the States.

Even as a boy, Lee exhibited the qualities that made the man. "He was a most exemplary student," said Lee's Quaker teacher in Alexandria. "He was never behind-time in his studies; never failed a single recitation; was perfectly observant of the rules and regulations of the institution; was gentle, manly, unobtrusive, and respectful in all his deportment to his teachers and his fellow students." Lee's "specialty was finishing up."

In 1825, Lee landed at West Point, where he made his first marks as a man. He had grown into a good-looking specimen, about six feet tall, with black hair. ("The handsomest man I ever saw," a British journalist said.) Word was, Lee was the best-looking man in the army. After four years, he graduated second in his class and without one demerit. Thus graduated an engineer, Lee's martial exploits began in the thick of battle in Mexico, under the command of Gen. Winfield Scott. In the war against Santa Anna, he distinguished himself as an engineer and a scout.

During the siege of Vera Cruz in March 1847, Lee and Lt. P. G. T. Beauregard surprised an American sentry and were nearly shot to death. The pistol bullet zinged between Lee's left arm and his body. "A deviation of a fraction of an inch in the soldier's aim," biographer Freeman wrote, "would have changed some very important chapters in American history." In the proximate future, it would have erased Lee's future as a hero in Mexico, first at Vera Cruz in assembling the artillery batteries with which Scott laid siege to the city.

At Cerro Gordo, Lee made his name by reconnoitering for Scott's army. Furtively scouting the terrain around a hill, the site of Mexican batteries, as well as nearby Rio Del Plan, Lee wound up behind enemy lines. He was traversing a path near a spring when he heard Spanish voices and quickly dropped behind a log near the water where the Mexicans came to drink. Undergrowth around the log concealed the tall Virginian, and the Mexicans, discussing the Americans confronting them, sat down on the log just three feet away. One even stepped over the log, but the engineer never moved. He waited hours, until dark, then crept back to his lines with a report. Lee led troops back to the area around Santa Anna's left, a movement that led to a rout of the Mexicans and the near capture of Santa Anna.

Wrote Scott, "I cannot refrain from bearing testimony to the intrepid coolness and gallantry exhibited by Captain Lee."

Lee shone again at Padierna and Churubusco, when he crossed a perilous lava field known as the Pedregal. He found a road across it, and the next morning, he led a detachment of five hundred men, under the command of Gen. Gideon Pillow, across the field to lay siege to Padierna. Lee participated in the battle, then carried messages back to Scott across the Pedregal through a driving rain around immense blocks of lava and across ravines, with "nothing to guide him but his singularly developed sense of direction," Freeman wrote, "and an occasional glimpse of the hill of Zacatepec when the lightning flashed." Scott was in this town, but when Lee arrived, the intended recipient of his intelligence had gone to San Augustin. Weary and soaked, Lee carried on to meet his commander. He next undertook a mission at midnight, across the same ground, to escort Gen. David E. Twiggs to the headquarters of Brig. Gen. Franklin Pierce.

The scouting was preparatory to the battle of Churubusco, where Lee distinguished himself again and which the Americans won. When it ended, Lee had been walking or riding for thirty-six hours, had thrice crossed the Pedregal, and had fought in three actions. Scott said that Lee's work was "the greatest feat of physical and moral courage, performed by any individual, to my knowledge, pending the campaign."

Lee led reconnaissance parties again to learn the terrain around Chapultepec, then assembled many of the artillery batteries with which Scott's forces laid siege to the city. After that, he guided an infantry party and eventually fainted, having gone nearly three days without sleep. Such was his mettle and devotion to duty. Uniformly, superior and fellow officers praised his grit and coolness under fire. But his commander's words are the best estimate of Lee. Scott's "success in Mexico," the general wrote, "was largely due to the skill, valor and undaunted energy of Robert E. Lee." He called Lee the "greatest military genius in America, the best soldier that I ever saw in the field." Continued Scott, "I tell you that if I were on my death bed tomorrow, and the president of the United States would tell me that a great battle was to be fought for the liberty or slavery of the country, and asked my judgment as to the ability of a commander, I would say with my dying breath, let it be Robert E. Lee."

Lee's fight in Mexico ended with his promotion to colonel. He continued his career in the army, landing at different posts. He was in Texas when states began seceding from the Union.

In victory or defeat, Robert E. Lee was magnanimous and humble. When his stalwart troops carried the day at Fredericksburg in December 1863, he scanned the fields that showed tremendous Federal losses and said, "It is well that war is so terrible, else we should grow too fond of it."

MAGNANIMOUS SERVICE, RECONCILIATION

THIS TREATMENT of Lee avoids detailing his role in the great cataclysm that ended, sadly, with the destruction of our constitutional order in April 1865. Superseding the tactics he employed at Fredericksburg and Chancellorsville, or the uncertainties and questions about his decisions at Gettysburg, are a few stories about Lee the man: how he conducted himself during the strife.

Lee's decision to fight for Virginia is one. Before George B. McClellan, George Gordon Meade, Ambrose E. Burnside, or Ulysses S. Grant became giants of the Yankee army, there was Lee. In 1860, Lee was considered the finest officer in the army, although he was not a general officer. On April 18, 1861, Lincoln's top aide, Francis Blair, invited Colonel Lee to a meeting. Blair offered Lee command of the federal army, buttressed with seventy-five thousand troops to be called up by the president. Lee declined Blair, most likely the most powerful man in America next to Lincoln. He would not draw his sword against his home and his people, against Virginia. Lee was first and foremost a loyal citizen of the Old Dominion. After meeting with Blair, Lee went to Scott, who again thought Lee the finest soldier in America. Lee, Scott said, must resign immediately.

Across the river at Arlington, Lee pondered his decision. His wife, Mary, remembered him pacing the floor. A few times, she thought, she heard him fall to his knees in prayer, asking

One of Lee's greatest virtues was his humility. He always credited God for his victories, such as his unlikely triumph at Chancellorsville in May 1863 (below). Yet when the Confederates failed, as they did at Gettysburg two months later, he heaped blame upon himself. "It's all my fault," he said. "I alone am to blame."

God to guide him. Lee was not a Secessionist, and he thought slavery was a moral evil. But he could not, he knew, draw his sword against his native soil, as he explained in a letter to his sister: "With all my devotion to the Union and the feeling of loyalty and duty of an American citizen, I have not been able to make up my mind to raise my hand against my relatives, my children, my home. I have therefore resigned my commission in the Army, and save in defence of my native state, with the sincere hope that my poor services may never be needed, I hope I may never be called upon to draw my sword."

Lee's decision wasn't just the end of a career, it was the end of his home, a home pervaded by the revenant of George Washington. Arlington became enemy territory when the war began, and the Lees fled deep into Virginia for the remainder of the war, never to return. So angry was Union Quarter-master Gen. Montgomery Meigs at what he considered Lee's treason and treachery (and also by the death of his son in battle) that he buried Union dead around the house, thus beginning the American Necropolis, Arlington National Cemetery.

In victory or defeat, Lee was magnanimous and humble. When his stalwart troops carried the day, he gave the glory to God. When they lost at Gettysburg, he took the blame. "It's all my fault," he said, and "I alone am to blame. A younger and more abler man than myself can be obtained." But he also understood that "in the good providence of God failure often proves a blessing."

"Thy will be done" was Lee's maxim. At Gettysburg, he demonstrated what it meant to be a Christian officer and gentlemen. Not far from Cemetery Ridge, a Yankee soldier lay wounded with a shattered left leg. Lee and his officers rode by, and the soldier, "a most bitter anti-South man," recognizing the most famous man below the Mason-Dixon Line, shouted "Hurrah for Union." Remembered the Union boy:

The General heard me, looked, stopped his horse, dismounted and came toward me. I must confess I at first thought he meant to kill me. But as he came up he looked down at me with such a sad expression upon his face that all fear left me, and I wondered what he was about. He extended his hand to me, grasping mine firmly, and looking right into my eyes, said: "My son, I hope you will soon be well." If I live to be a thousand years I shall never forget the expression on General Lee's face. There he was defeated, retiring from a field that had cost him and his cause almost their last hope, and yet he stopped to say words like those to a wounded soldier of the opposition who had taunted him as he passed by! As soon as the General had left me, I cried myself to sleep there upon the bloody ground.

Lee surrendered at Appomattox Court House because he understood that continuing the bloody war was futile. He gave up the struggle humbly, knowing that the best interests of his country lay in reconciliation, and he discouraged talk of guerrilla warfare and permanent discord.

"Madam," he told a grieving but spiteful Confederate widow after the war, "do not train up your children in hostility to the Government of the United States. Remember that we are one country now. Dismiss from your mind all sectional feeling, and bring them up to be Americans." After the war, in accepting the presidency of Washington College in Lexington, Lee wrote again of reconciliation. "It is the duty of every citizen . . . to do all in his power to aid in the restoration of peace and harmony."

Lee expected Southerners to restore peace and treat Northerners, including former Federal soldiers, courteously. Once, when it was rumored that General Grant would visit the Greenbrier, a young woman asked what Lee would do. For Lee, only one answer was possible. "If General Grant comes," he replied, "I shall welcome him to my home, and show him all the courtesy which is due from one gentlemen to another."

On another occasion, a soldier landed at the gate of his home, talked for a few minutes, and went away "well pleased," Freeman wrote. Coincidentally, a pastor of the Baptist church and college chaplain walked up, whereupon Lee remarked, "That is one of our old soldiers who is in necessitous circum-stances." When the "wholly unreconstructed" pastor inquired after the Confederate command for which the poor man had fought, Lee replied, "He fought on the other side, but we must not remember that against him now." Later, that Union vet-eran, like other Northerners, remembered Lee as "the noblest man that ever lived." Lee "not only had a kind word for an old soldier who had fought against him, but he gave me some money to help me on my way."

Lee fully demonstrated what reconciliation meant, not just by denouncing "bitter expressions against the North and [the] United States government" as "undignified and unbecoming," but by a deed of remarkable moral courage at St. Paul's Episco-pal Church in Richmond. When the minister announced com-munion, a black man stood first, then walked up the altar and knelt in his Sunday finery. The congregation was stunned, and the congregants kept to their seats in "solemn silence," accord-ing to one account, and the minister was embarrassed. They believed it was an attempt to embarrass the congregants with a symbolic, undeclared avowal that the regime of the Old South had ended. But then Lee rose and knelt next to the man, his example a silent reproach to the assembly.

Humility, Honor, and Duty

In accepting the post at the college, Lee again demonstrated his deeply ingrained and lifelong humility. He said, "I have feared that I should be unable to discharge its duties to the satisfaction of the trustees or to the benefit of the country. The proper education of youth require not only great ability, but I fear more strength than I now possess."

But Lee had always been a humble man. When the secession convention in Virginia appointed him commander of the state's army and navy, he said he was "not prepared . . . I would have much preferred had your choice fallen on an abler man." One wonders whom that would have been. Lee once told a would-be biographer who requested an interview, "I know of nothing good I could tell you of myself." And to Jefferson Davis, he once wrote, "I have no complaints to make of anyone but myself."

Even in a letter to his wife in 1863, Lee's humility spoke out: "I tremble for our country when I hear of the confidence expressed in me. I know too well my weakness, and that our only hope is in God." Just before his death, on a tour of the South, crowds of admirers awaited his every stop, much as the soldiers who followed him into battle cheered him as he rode through their ranks. But Lee was ever humble. "Why should they care to see me?" he asked. "I am only a poor old Confederate."

"Never," as Marshall Fishwick wrote in *Lee After the War,* did Lee "scramble for favor." Although still a captain twenty-one years after leaving West Point, "he would not push his case" for promotion. "I know how those things are awarded at Washington, and how the President will be besieged by claimants. I do not wish to be numbered among them." And "when a subordinate asked about promotions," Lee replied, 'What do you care about rank? I would serve under a corporal if necessary.'" Asked why he never wore the insignia of his full rank, Lee replied, "I do not care for display. The rank of colonel is about as high as I ought ever to have gotten."

On April 9, 1865, Lee negotiated the surrender of his army to U. S. Grant and received very generous terms, even food for his starving men. Back at his camp, he told his soldiers, "Go home now, and if you make as good citizens as you have soldiers, you will do well, and I shall always be proud of you."

At the college, his mission, a reprise of his superintendency at West Point, was uncomplicated. Lee wouldn't just instruct his charges academically but morally and religiously as well. He knew the students by name and the grades they made and could recite them from memory. He once corrected a professor on one pupil's mathematics grade. He gently remonstrated with young men who fell behind in their studies. But as a man whose guide was the Bible and who was charged with the formation of a young man's future, his maxim was simple. "If I could only know that all the young men in the college were good Christians," said he, "I should have nothing more to desire. I dread the thought of any student going away from the college without becoming a sincere Christian." At

Washington College, Lee attended chapel daily, another example for the men he would send into the world.

His renown was such that businessmen sought to profit by his name, but Lee, having accepted a mission to educate young men, refused their blandishments. On one occasion, he refused ten thousand dollars to act as titular head of an insurance company. "I cannot consent to receive pay," he answered, "for service I do not render." He turned down a fifty-thousand-dollar salary from a English businessman: "I cannot leave my present position. I have a self-imposed task. I have led the young men of the South in battle. I must teach their sons to discharge their duty in life."

Lee's gift to us is his example, his dedication to duty, his humility, his self-denial, and his faith. He practiced what he preached; he set an example for his sons and daughters and instructed them in the timeless truths that inspire right reason

Lee refused to profit from his fame and reputation after the war. He turned down lucrative job offers to become president of Washington College. There, he said, "I have a self-imposed task. I have led the young men of the South in battle. I must teach their sons to discharge their duty in life."

DEFEAT IS NOT DISHONOR

and a Christian life that would get them to heaven. He left many of his maxims in letters to his children, students at West Point and Washington College, and fellow officers.

Having commanded men in battle and in the classroom, Lee understood that forming a man's character requires teaching a man, at an early age, how to react to the evils of the world, not to avoid any contact with them. This is why he emphasized Christian living among his students at Washington College. Jesus Christ, he knew, would provide a man with the sword, buckler, and shield he needed to oppose evil if we would only let him. "Young men must not expect to escape contact with evil," he said, "but must learn not to be contaminated by it." Avoiding contamination requires discipline, and thus did he offer what could be called a first commandment to any of his students: "Study hard, be always a gentlemen, live cleanly and remember God." No one can neglect to study the Bible, he thought; we must understand that no matter what happens in life, "God disposes," and "this ought to satisfy us."

Arising from his admonition to be a good Christian were his corollary principles regarding obedience, duty, and how a man should treat not just his friends but those he might consider enemies.

Thus one of Lee's principal topics was obedience to just authority and, following that, doing one's duty. Being a military man and knowing that following the orders of those who know better can mean life or death, Lee said that real men are obedient to the authority under which they place themselves voluntarily. "You cannot be a true man," he said, "unless you learn to obey." Indeed, in obedience to those God places over us, we can learn to conduct ourselves. Lee knew that and acted accordingly.

Yet obedience wasn't just the sign of manhood, it was one's duty not only to persons in authority but also to God. Thus was *duty* another word we find Lee using time and time again. "Do your duty," the general said. "That is all the pleasure, all the comfort, all the glory we can enjoy in this world." Yet Lee also knew that doing one's duty must be voluntary, that a real man not only does his duty but also does it willingly, because it is right.

Doing right was always on Lee's mind, and he did not believe, as so many people believe today, that doing wrong can be good. "I am opposed to the theory of doing wrong that good may come of it," he said. "You must act right whatever the consequences." We should never do something wrong to make or keep a friend, he wrote, and he also knew that "if you don't behave as you believe," as Archbishop Fulton Sheen said, "you will end by believing as you behave." "Private and public life are subject to the same rules," he said, perhaps anticipating modern men and women who say that what a public official does privately does not affect his conduct publicly. "And truth and manliness are two qualities," he continued, "that will carry you through this world much better than policy, or tact, or expediency, or any other word that was ever devised to conceal or mystify a deviation from a straight line." Simply put, Lee said he was "unwilling to do that which is wrong."

This isn't to say Lee was perfect. He wasn't. But he strove for perfection each and every waking moment. He seemed completely unaffected by any of the seven cardinal sins— pride, sloth, envy, avarice, lust, gluttony, and anger—and embodied the seven virtues—prudence, temperance, justice, fortitude, faith, hope, and charity.

Particularly notable is Lee's strict attention to the golden rule: do unto others as you would have them to do unto you. Among his principles in this matter was that being a good Christian was "the most important thing." From there, Lee repeats the advice St. Francis gave: do not dispute others or give

Said British Field Marshal Viscount Wolseley, Lee was "the most perfect man I ever met. . . . I have met many of the great men of my time, but Lee alone impressed me with the feeling that I was in the presence of a man who was cast in a grander mold, and made of different and finer metal than other men."

injury to them. "We should live so as to say and do nothing to the injury of any one," Lee said. "It is not only best as a matter of principle, but it is the path to peace and honor." He said we must judge adversaries from their point of view, not our own, if we want to understand them, and someone who may not agree with us isn't always an enemy. And if a man does find fault with another, he must have the courage to confront him personally: "If you have any fault to find with any one, tell him, not others, of what you complain; there is no more dangerous experiment than that of undertaking to be one thing before a man's face and another behind his back."

Lee was the embodiment of what it meant to be a Christian gentlemen, and as his biographer observed, he was one of the

After the war, many tried to reinterpret its outcome. A significant part of that effort was an emphasis on Lee as a stolid commander surrounded by gifted generals who led outnumbered armies to unlikely victories. Lee, however, refused to speak of the war or second-guess himself or his lieutenants.

few great men "in whom there is no inconsistency to be explained, no enigma to be solved. What he seemed, he was—a wholly human gentlemen." John Henry Cardinal Newman, a nineteenth-century British prelate, said that a gentlemen, by definition, never inflicts pain. The words applied to Lee, who understood the nature of power and how to wield it and the responsibilities with which God and nature charge the powerful. Newman's idea is found in Lee's description of a gentlemen:

> The forbearing use of power does not only form a touchstone; but the manner in which an individual enjoys certain advantages over others, is a test of a true gentleman. The power which the strong have over the weak, the magistrate over the

citizen, the employer over the employed, the educated over the unlettered, the experienced over the confiding, even the clever over the silly; the forbearing and inoffensive use of all this power or authority, or a total abstinence from it when the case admits it, will show the gentleman in a plain light. The gentleman does not needlessly and unnecessarily remind an offender of a wrong he may have committed against him. He cannot only forgive, he can forget; and he strives for that nobleness of self and mildness of character, which imparts sufficient strength to let the past be but the past. A true man of honor feels humbled himself when he cannot help humbling others.

Unsurprisingly, Lee was admired not just by the men who served under him but by those who opposed him in battle. He was beloved by all Americans, North and South, for the example he set not only in victory but also in defeat. Yankees wrote of him admiringly, seeing in Lee a man for the ages, and knowing God had created a peerless human being. "Never had mother a nobler son," opined the *New York Herald* the day after Lee died. "In him, all that was pure and lofty found lodgment. . . . He conquered us in misfortune by the grand manner in which he sustained himself. . . . And for such a man we are all tears and sorrow today."

"When the future historian shall come to survey the character of Lee " said Benjamin H. Hill to the Southern Historical Society in 1874, "he will find it rising like a huge mountain above the undulating plane of humanity, and he must lift his eyes high toward heaven to catch its summit."

Lee possessed every virtue of other great commanders without their vices. He was a foe without hate, a friend without treachery, a soldier without cruelty, a victor without oppression, and a victim without murmuring. He was a public officer without vices, a private citizen without wrong, a neighbor without re-proach, a Christian without hypocrisy, and a man without guile. He was a Caesar without his ambition, Frederick with-out his tyranny, Napoleon without his selfishness, and Wash-ington without his reward. He was obedient to authority as a servant, and royal in authority as a true king. He was gentle as a woman in life, modest and pure as a virgin in thought, watchful as a Roman vestal in duty, submissive to law as Socrates, and grand in battle as Achilles.

In today's cynical world, such an encomium seems a bit much, but our world is the world of the antihero. A century ago, such wasn't the case. When Lee died, the nation mourned, North and South having agreed that, despite the war, Southern war-riors would take their place in the pantheon of American he-roes. Americans, even Yankees, knew what Lee symbolized, and they admired him, his loyalty to Virginia and the South notwithstanding.

Union Gen. Morris Schaff, present at the surrender of Lee's forces at Appomattox Court House in April 1865, remem-bered the indelible impression left by Lee:

He was one who, though famous, was not honeycombed with ambition or tainted with cunning or cant, and though a soldier and wearing soldier's laurels, yet never craved nor sought hon-ors except as they bloomed on deeds done for the glory of his lawfully constituted authority; in short a soldier to whom the sense of duty was a gospel and a man of the world whose only rule in life was that life should [be] upright and stainless. I cannot but think Providence meant, through him, to prolong the ideal of the gentlemen in the world. It is easy to see why Lee has become the embodiment of the one of the world's ideals, that of the soldier, the Christian and the gentleman.

And from the bottom of my heart I thank Heaven . . . for the comfort of having a character like Lee's to look at.

Schaff's experience was not unique. Lee's aura was nearly angelic, his presence, even for friends, awesome. Lee was on a long horseback ride with Capt. James J. White, his closest friend in Lexington. Nightfall forced them to take lodgings in a farmhouse, and the two were required to share a bed. White, however, couldn't bring himself to do so. He said sleeping with the Archangel Gabriel would be easier than sleeping with Lee, with whom "no man was great enough to be intimate."

Said British Field Marshal Viscount Wolseley, Lee was "the most perfect man I ever met. . . . I have met many of the great

Lee's example in victory and defeat inspired all. He was, one admirer said, "a Caesar without his ambition; Frederick [the Great] without his tyranny; Napoleon without his selfishness; and Washington without his reward. . . . As grand in battle as Achilles."

men of my time, but Lee alone impressed me with the feeling that I was in the presence of a man who was cast in a grander mold, and made of different and finer metal than other men."

Lee *was* cast in a grander mold and made of finer metal; he was a knight whose armor was fired and polished over seven

---

Robert E. Lee left thousands of words of wisdom in letters and notes. Many of them are worth committing to memory:

You cannot be a true man unless you learn to obey.

Study hard, be always a gentleman,
live cleanly and remember God.

Do your duty. That is all the pleasure, all the
comfort, all the glory we can enjoy in this world.

We must all try to be good Christians.
That is the most important thing.

As a general principle, you should not force young
men to do their duty, but let them do it voluntarily
and thereby develop their characters.

Private and public life are subject to the same rules;
and truth and manliness are two qualities that
will carry you through this world much better
than policy, or tact, or expediency, or any
other word that was ever devised to conceal
or mystify a deviation from a straight line.

God disposes. This ought to satisfy us.

Never do a wrong thing to make a
friend or to keep one.

No one ever becomes too old to study
the precious truths of the Bible.

---

hundred years of history, beginning at the battle of Hastings. Unsurprisingly, Mary Lee agreed: "A more upright and conscientious Christian never lived." Few if any men have received such testimonials from best friends and wives, much less former foes in battle.

I am opposed to the theory of doing wrong that good may come of it. . . . [Y]ou must act right whatever the consequences.

We should live so as to say and do nothing to the injury of any one. It is not only best as a matter of principle, but it is the path to peace and honor.

Be strictly honorable in every act, and be not ashamed to do right. Acknowledge right to be your aim and strive to reach it.

The better rule is to judge our adversaries from their standpoint, not from ours.

Those who oppose our purposes are not always to be regarded as our enemies.

Young men must not expect to escape contact with evil, but must learn not to be contaminated by it.

There is a true glory and a true honor: The glory of duty done—the honor of the integrity of principle.

If you have any fault to find with any one, tell him, not others, of what you complain; there is no more dangerous experiment than that of undertaking to be one thing before a man's face and another behind his back.

I am unwilling to do what is wrong.

Lee was another of the men in these pages who externalized everything opposed to what many men represent today: the self-indulgent, the feminized, the haughty, the weak, the undisciplined. Indeed, Lee the Christian is anathema to almost all the attributes with which modern society imbues its young men. E. Michael Jones, the editor of *Culture Wars* magazine, wrote about the modern "culture of appetite," the apologists for which aver that men and women may indulge any lust imaginable with a clean conscience. Lee was the antipode of such a person, which is what made him a real man in the most profound sense of those words.

In 1870, Lee's meritorious life closed. Like Jackson, on his deathbed, Lee called upon A. P. Hill to engage the enemy. "Tell Hill he must come up." As Lee "crossed over the river to lie under the shade of the trees," to quote Thomas J. "Stonewall" Jackson's last words, he uttered a final order: "Strike the tent." Thus ended the life of our greatest American, a man who lived the venerable code of the Christian gentlemen. In Lee, we see all that is noble, gentle, kind, loving, faithful, loyal, and courageous.

Lee teaches us what it means to be a real man.

AFTERWORD

Having read this book, a critic might ask whether it suggests that society cannot create real men such as these.

No. Society can and does create real men. But we see few of them in books or movies because the virtues that make men heroic are anathema to modern society. We may see them in the news, but if they have not adopted modern feminist ideology, it will be held against them as "old-fashioned." The real men we meet are real not because of society but in spite of it. The culture at large punishes real men for holding beliefs, voicing opinions, and doing deeds deemed beyond the pale; that is, the politically incorrect things that offend the feminist sisterhood and its submissive stable of eunuchs, that suggest God endowed men and women with different gifts that enable them to play different but equally important and complementary roles.

A healthy society would raise boys and girls accordingly. But modern society is unhealthy. It says the sexes are identical. This is obviously untrue to average people or anyone intellectually unharmed by a doctorate from a major university. But average people don't run things. The political, social, and cultural elites run things, meaning the politicians, grade-school teachers, university professors, social workers, writers, business and Hollywood executives, doctors and lawyers, etc.

These are the so-called experts. In sixty short years since World War II, they have convinced a significant portion of the population that the sexes are interchangeable. As one sociologist expressed it, the experts have taught us that men are just big women, and women are just little men. To the degree the sexes are not identical, they claim, the culture and laws must be remade to erase the divinely endowed attributes that are natural, beautiful, and unique. And, of course, necessary to a healthy society.

The question is where and how this lesson is taught. It begins in the home, with confused or weak parents, but it reaches a level of persistent and persuasive propaganda in public schools and popular entertainment. Some of the key documentation of the anti-male zeitgeist comes not from outraged men but from concerned women who wonder what kind of timber society is raising. They include social critics such as Christina Hoff Somers, who wrote *The War Against Boys,* and Diane Ravitch, a historian of education. Five minutes of digging on the Internet unearths reams of material that discloses what schools are doing to boys.

With an extensive set of links and sources, Illinoisloop.org, for instance, posts a list of twenty-two practices in grade schools that harm boys in myriad ways. Where the subject matter of genuine manhood is concerned, the site scrutinizes curricula and makes several observations. "Assigned literature," it noted, "is skewed lopsidedly towards social issues, and away from novels of high adventure, courage, patriotism, etc." And boys also face an "almost total absence of fact-based biography and non-fiction in literature and reading classes."

The idea is that a high-school boy is much more likely to read and enjoy *The Killer Angels,* a novel about the battle of Gettysburg, or a biography of Gen. George S. Patton, than *The Color Purple,* a novel about the tearful travails of a put-upon black woman, or the dreary doggerel of Maya Angelou. If you're going to give a boy poetry, give him Robert W. Service, who wrote masculine, exciting tales about the frontier such as "The Cremation of Sam McGee" or "The Shooting of Dan McGrew." Today, Service is truly one of "The Men That Don't Fit In," as one of his poems is titled.

Grade-school boys should not read stories and watch movies about girls who make the football team or boys who thrive in ballet. They should not read or watch material that subtly, or perhaps not so subtly, scorns normal feelings: the burning desire to compete vigorously and emerge victorious, the aspiration to become a champion. They should read stories for boys. To cite just one example, they can try the venerable Landmark biographies and tales (from Random House) about Stonewall Jackson, Robert E. Lee, and Custer's last stand, among others, which portray heroism and adventure and fire the imagination. They should read about Daniel Boone and David Crockett, Jesse James and Wyatt Earp, Audie Murphy and George S. Patton. Indeed, Patton viscerally understood men and how to motivate them. Men, he said, naturally worship heroes. So do boys. In his speech to the Third Army before the invasion of Normandy, Patton put on his "war face" and delivered some simple truths: "Americans love to fight—traditionally! All real Americans love the sting and clash of battle. When you were kids, you all admired the champion marble player, the fastest runner, the big-league ball players, the toughest boxers." Thus should boys read about the men in these pages.

Boys need heroes to emulate, but commentators such as Ravitch have argued that the schools, and society at large, won't permit them. Reading material, she said, has been feminized. In her article "Education and the Culture Wars," published in *Daedalus, Journal of the American Academy of Arts and*

Sciences, Ravitch described reviewing test material as one of the board members of a federal agency. She learned that reading selections on one standardized test were not only racially biased against whites but also sexually biased against boys. "In one story, a white boy in a difficult situation weeps and says plaintively, 'If only my big sister were here, I would know what to do.'" Ravitch also reviewed one publisher's guidelines for standardized tests: Among the taboo items were:

> Men shown as "strong, brave, and silent," women shown as "weepy, fearful, and emotional"; boys playing sports, or girls playing with dolls; . . . men working as lawyers, doctors, or plumbers; women working as nurses or secretaries; . . . men playing sports or working with tools; women cooking and caring for children; . . . men portrayed as breadwinners; women portrayed as homemakers. . . . Illustrators must not use pink for baby girls or blue for baby boys. Out is the old-fashioned idea that females care more about their appearance than males do: today's illustrator must portray both sexes "preening in front of a mirror," with Dad using a blow-dryer.

Thus is a metrosexual made, but in any event Ravitch and others aren't just describing obvious propaganda. They are describing the cultural elite's manipulation and alteration of traditional symbols to remake boys and reorder society. By replacing those traditional symbols, they have changed the moral order from what it was fifty years ago to what is now. The entertainment industry, particularly films, has played a key role in this effort, given the ideology of those who run and work in it. An unsubtle example of their manipulating symbols is *Brokeback Mountain,* the film about two homosexual cowboys whose heroism lies in surrendering to their unnatural lust.

Question is, why cowboys? Why not two florists, two beauticians, or two interior decorators? Because these professions are not equated with raw masculinity.

The cowboy has forever symbolized strength and masculinity. He works hard, plays hard, and fights for what's right. He typifies integrity, humility, reverence, and courage. He personifies the real man. So the film was a cultural watershed, not because it celebrates perversion, but because it malevolently continues what the leftist cultural elite sees as an indispensable tactic in their strategy to subvert the Christian moral order: to replace the traditional symbols of our culture with its own. Once accepted, those symbols are invulnerable to reproach. If cowboys, who are real men, can be homosexuals, then anyone can, which in turn means those cowboys immunize homosexual sodomy from society's normal and natural opprobrium. And *Brokeback* is of a piece with other films that would replace traditional symbols of masculinity with new ones, such as the woman Navy Seal portrayed in *G.I. Jane* or the heroic lady captain in *Courage Under Fire* in which men are depicted as incapable of martial valor and success without the help, direction, or inspiration of women.

To stop the subversion, we must change what our children see as "normal," which is most of what popular culture presents. We must flatly and without reservation reject the feminist ethos. We must change what they read and see. One change would be giving kids good literature and the kind of history in this book. The material is out there for kids of all ages. But cast adrift in a veritable ocean of lies and propaganda, parents have a tough time paddling against the current. Success will require some of the same strength, tenacity, and grit that inspired the heroic deeds of these ten courageous Americans we should know and admire.

SOURCES

Chapter 1: Francis Marion

Bass, Robert D. *Swamp Fox: The Life and Campaigns of General Francis Marion.* New York: Holt, 1959.

James, William Dobein. *A Sketch of the Life of Brig. Gen. Francis Marion, and a History of His Brigade, From Its Rise in June, 1780, Until Disbanded in December, 1782.* Charleston, SC: Gould and Riley, 1821.

Rankin, Hugh F. *Francis Marion: The Swamp Fox.* New York: Crowell, 1973.

Simms, William Gilmore. *The Life of Francis Marion.* N.p., 1844.

Chapter 2: Eddie Rickenbacker

Fitzpatrick, James K. *Builders of the American Dream.* New Rochelle, NY: Arlington House, 1977.

Rickenbacker, Eddie. *Fighting the Flying Circus.* New York: Stokes, 1919.

———. *Seven Came Through.* Garden City, NY: Doubleday, Doran, 1943.

Chapter 3: Vince Lombardi

Maraniss, David. *When Pride Still Mattered: A Life of Vince Lombardi.* New York: Simon & Schuster, 1999.

www.vincelombardi.com.

Chapter 4: Rocky Versace

Medal of Honor Recommendation for Capt. Humbert Roque Versace. A staff study prepared by Duane E. Frederic, August 28, 1999.

U.S. Army Ranger Hall of Fame. Nomination Letter for Capt. Humbert R. Versace, September 12, 2000.

Vogel, Steve. "Honoring the Defiant One." *Washington Post,* May 27, 2001.

———. "A Mission Inspired by a POW's Persistence." *Washington Post,* July 8, 2002.

Warren, Tim. "Never Give In." *The Washingtonian,* March 2000.

Chapter 5: James Butler "Wild Bill" Hickok

Rosa, Joseph G. *Wild Bill Hickok: The Man and His Myth.* Lawrence: University of Kansas Press, 1996.

Wilstach, Frank J. *Wild Bill Hickok: The Prince of Pistoleers.* Garden City, NY: Doubleday Page & Co., 1926.

Richard, John. "Chronology on the Life of James Butler 'Wild Bill' Hickok," http://www.kansasheritage.org/gunfighters/JBH.html.

Chapter 6: Lou Gehrig

Bak, Richard. *Lou Gehrig: An American Classic.* Dallas: Taylor, 1995.

Gehrig, Eleanor, and Joseph Durso. *My Luke and I.* New York: Crowell, 1976.

Robinson, Ray. *Iron Horse: Lou Gehrig in His Time.* New York: Norton, 1990.

Chapter 7: Audie Murphy

Graham, Don. *No Name on the Bullet: A Biography of Audie Murphy.* New York: Viking, 1989.

Murphy, Audie. *To Hell and Back.* New York: Holt, 1949.

Reeder, Red. *Medal of Honor Heroes.* New York: Random House, 1965.

The Audie L. Murphy Memorial Website, http://audiemurphy.com.

CHAPTER 8: DAVID CROCKETT

Abbott, John S. C. *David Crockett: His Life and Adventures.* New York: Dodd & Mead, 1874.

Davis, William C. *Three Roads to the Alamo: The Lives and Fortunes of David Crockett, James Bowie, and William Barret Travis.* New York: HarperCollins, 1998.

Ellis, Edward S. *The Life of Colonel David Crockett: Comprising His Adventures as Backwoodsman and Hunter.* Philadelphia: Porter & Coates, 1884.

McGrath, Roger. "In Search of Rawhide Heroes." *American Conservative,* June 7, 2004.

Shackford, James Atkins. *David Crockett: The Man and the Legend.* Chapel Hill: University of North Carolina Press, 1956.

CHAPTER 9: ANDREW JACKSON

Booraem, Hendrik. *Young Hickory: The Making of Andrew Jackson.* Dallas: Taylor Publishing, 2001.

Remini, Robert V. *Andrew Jackson and His Indian Wars.* New York: Viking, 2001.

————. *Andrew Jackson and the Course of American Empire, 1767–1821.* New York: Harper & Row, 1977.

Schlesinger, Arthur M., Jr. *The Age of Jackson.* Boston: Little, Brown, 1945.

CHAPTER 10: ROBERT E. LEE

Fishwick, Marshall. *Lee After the War.* New York: Dodd, Mead, 1963.

Fontaine, William Winston. "The Descent of General Robert Edward Lee from Robert the Bruce, of Scotland." *Southern Historical Society Papers,* 1881.

Freeman, Douglas Southall. *R. E. Lee: A Biography.* 4 vols. New York: Scribner's, 1934–35.

Hamilton, J. G. de Roulhac. *The Life of Robert E. Lee for Young Gentlemen.* 1917. Reprint, Stuarts Draft, VA: Virginia Gentlemen Books, n.d.

Sources

Nagel, Paul C. *The Lees of Virginia: Seven Generations of an American Family.* New York: Oxford University Press, 1990.

Williams, Richard G., ed. *The Maxims of Robert E. Lee for Young Gentlemen.* Fairfax, VA: Xulon Press, 2002.

INDEX

Index